Steroid Abuse

by Tamara L. Roleff

LUCENT BOOKS
A part of Gale, Cengage Learning

GALE
CENGAGE Learning

Detroit • New York • San Francisco • New Haven, Conn • Waterville, Maine • London

LIBRARY OF CONGRESS CATALOGING-IN-PUBLICATION DATA

Roleff, Tamara L., 1959–
Steroid abuse / by Tamara L. Roleff.
    p. cm. -- (Hot topics)
Includes bibliographical references and index.
ISBN 978-1-4205-0229-9 (hardcover)
1. Steroid abuse. I. Title.
HV5822.S68.R65 2010
362.29'6--dc22

2009040811

Lucent Books
27500 Drake Rd.
Farmington Hills, MI 48331

ISBN-13: 978-1-4205-0229-9
ISBN-10: 1-4205-0229-8

Printed in the United States of America
1 2 3 4 5 6 7 14 13 12 11 10
Printed by Bang Printing, Brainerd, MN, 1st Ptg., 02/2010

CONTENTS

FOREWORD   4

INTRODUCTION   6
A Commonly Used Drug

CHAPTER 1   11
A Short History of the Use of Steroids in Sports

CHAPTER 2   26
Why Use Steroids?

CHAPTER 3   42
Is It Cheating to Use Steroids?

CHAPTER 4   55
Regulating Steroid Use

CHAPTER 5   74
What Is the Future of Steroids in Sports?

NOTES   89

DISCUSSION QUESTIONS   95

ORGANIZATIONS TO CONTACT   97

FOR MORE INFORMATION   101

INDEX   105

PICTURE CREDITS   111

ABOUT THE AUTHOR   112

FOREWORD

Young people today are bombarded with information. Aside from traditional sources such as newspapers, television, and the radio, they are inundated with a nearly continuous stream of data from electronic media. They send and receive e-mails and instant messages, read and write online "blogs," participate in chat rooms and forums, and surf the Web for hours. This trend is likely to continue. As Patricia Senn Breivik, the former dean of university libraries at Wayne State University in Detroit, has stated, "Information overload will only increase in the future. By 2020, for example, the available body of information is expected to double every 73 days! How will these students find the information they need in this coming tidal wave of information?"

Ironically, this overabundance of information can actually impede efforts to understand complex issues. Whether the topic is abortion, the death penalty, gay rights, or obesity, the deluge of fact and opinion that floods the print and electronic media is overwhelming. The news media report the results of polls and studies that contradict one another. Cable news shows, talk radio programs, and newspaper editorials promote narrow viewpoints and omit facts that challenge their own political biases. The World Wide Web is an electronic minefield where legitimate scholars compete with the postings of ordinary citizens who may or may not be well-informed or capable of reasoned argument. At times, strongly worded testimonials and opinion pieces both in print and electronic media are presented as factual accounts.

Conflicting quotes and statistics can confuse even the most diligent researchers. A good example of this is the question of whether or not the death penalty deters crime. For instance, one study found that murders decreased by nearly one-third when the death penalty was reinstated in New York in 1995. Death penalty supporters cite this finding to support their argument that the existence of the death penalty deters criminals from committing murder. However, another study found that states without the death penalty have murder rates below the national average. This study is cited by opponents of capital punishment, who reject the claim that the death penalty deters murder. Students need context and clear, informed discussion if they are to think critically and make informed decisions.

The Hot Topics series is designed to help young people wade through the glut of fact, opinion, and rhetoric so that they can think critically about controversial issues. Only by reading and thinking critically will they be able to formulate a viewpoint that is not simply the parroted views of others. Each volume of the series focuses on one of today's most pressing social issues and provides a balanced overview of the topic. Carefully crafted narrative, fully documented primary and secondary source quotes, informative sidebars, and study questions all provide excellent starting points for research and discussion. Full-color photographs and charts enhance all volumes in the series. With its many useful features, the Hot Topics series is a valuable resource for young people struggling to understand the pressing issues of the modern era.

INTRODUCTION

A COMMONLY USED DRUG

The sporting world was saddened, but not surprised, when it was revealed that another of baseball's greatest players had been caught taking a banned substance. Manny Ramirez, a twelve-time All-Star, World Series Most Valuable Player (MVP), and one of the game's best batters, tested positive for human chorionic gonadotropin (hCG) and was suspended for fifty games. While not a steroid itself, hCG is a female fertility drug that is typically used by steroid users to get their testosterone production started again after taking a cycle of steroids.

A Lax Organization

Major League Baseball (MLB) was one of the last sporting organizations to crack down on players who use performance-enhancing drugs. The steroid androstenedione was discovered in Mark McGwire's locker during his home run race with Sammy Sosa in 1998, but no action was taken against him because steroid use was not illegal in baseball at the time. After an anonymous survey of drug use among ballplayers in 2003 showed that 5 to 7 percent of baseball players used steroids, Major League Baseball finally banned steroids and performance-enhancing substances and enacted drug testing policies. Players who tested positive for steroids in 2004 were sent to a counselor. The following year, ballplayers were given a ten-game suspension, and twelve players—including Rafael Palmeiro, who five months earlier had testified before Congress, "I have never used steroids. Period."[1]— were suspended. In 2006 the suspension policy was changed again, this time to fifty games, and as of midway through the 2009 season, seventeen more players had been suspended. Ramirez is just the most recent—and perhaps greatest —of professional baseball players to be suspended for using a banned substance.

Confidentiality Is Breached

Despite promises of confidentiality and anonymity, the name of at least one player who tested positive in 2003 was leaked to the press in 2009. *Sports Illustrated* magazine revealed that Alex Rodriguez was one of 104 ballplayers who had tested positive for steroids in 2003. At first Rodriguez refused to confirm or deny the allegations, saying, "You'll have to talk to the union."[2] At the time Rodriguez failed this drug test, Major League Baseball prohibited players from using illegal drugs, including steroids, but

In February 2009 Alex Rodriguez read a statement to the media admitting that he used steroids while playing for the Texas Rangers.

did not have penalties in place for those who tested positive for drugs. A few days after his positive test result was leaked, Rodriguez admitted in an ESPN interview that he had been taking steroids during the years he had played for Texas. Rodriguez explained about the pressure he felt to live up to the standards expected of him and added: "Back then, [baseball] was a different culture. It was very loose. I was young. I was stupid. I was naïve. And I wanted to prove to everyone that I was worth being one of the greatest players of all time. I did take a banned substance. And for that, I am very sorry and deeply regretful."[3]

No such apology was forthcoming from Ramirez, however. As of mid-2009 Ramirez had refused to give any statements or explanations about why he was taking steroids, although he did apologize to his teammates a few weeks after he tested positive for steroids.

Steroids in Baseball

In his second book about steroids in baseball, *Vindicated: Big Names, Big Liars, and the Battle to Save Baseball*, former professional ballplayer and admitted steroid user Jose Canseco disputed Major League Baseball's figures of 5 to 7 percent steroid use among ballplayers. According to Canseco, in the whole clubhouse, indeed, practically the whole league, at least "80 percent or more,"[4] took steroids. Canseco wrote of injecting steroids into McGwire, Palmeiro, Juan Gonzalez, and Ivan Rodriguez, to name just a few. The atmosphere in the locker room was so loose and casual, Canseco wrote, that the ballplayers would talk candidly about which steroids they used and in what dosages. According to Canseco, "This was light conversation, and we never bothered to stop unless a reporter was around. By 1997, in front of anyone but the media, it was completely accepted that we would talk openly about steroids."[5]

Getting and Keeping the Edge

Canseco claims it is easy to determine who is using steroids. Ballplayers who suddenly bulk up and weigh 40 pounds (18kg) more at spring training than they did the previous fall are obvious candidates for steroid use, he asserts. Statistics also tell those in the know what the ballplayers have been doing. For example, Barry Bonds had hit forty-nine home runs in 2000. According to Canseco, Bonds started taking steroids at the end of the 2000 season, and the next year he hit seventy-three home runs, a Major League record that some claim is tainted because of the steroid use. Other ballplayers also posted impressive improvements in their averages. Mark McGwire hit thirty-nine home runs in 1995, fifty-eight in 1997, and had seventy in 1998. Sammy Sosa was close to doubling the number of home runs he hit in just one year, going from thirty-six home runs in 1997 to sixty-six in 1998.

One of the arguments against steroid use is that if a few players take steroids, then everyone will need to use steroids in order to remain competitive. According to Canseco and others like him, players need to take these performance-enhancing substances in order to keep their jobs: "The players weren't taking steroids because they enjoyed them, or because it was so much fun; they were taking them to keep up with the competition. Without steroids, many of them felt, not unjustifiably, that they would lose their edge. And without that edge, they felt, with great certainty, that they would lose their jobs."[6] Canseco says it was because he and a few other baseball stars started taking steroids that 80 percent or more of ballplayers ended up using performance-enhancing drugs. It became, he said, "the Steroid Era."[7]

The Mitchell Report

In order to find out how serious the problem of steroid use in baseball was, Baseball Commissioner Bud Selig asked former senator George J. Mitchell to study the issue. Mitchell released his report in December 2007, and he named nearly ninety current and former baseball players who used steroids. Steroids were a big threat to baseball, as Mitchell wrote: "The illegal use of performance-enhancing substances poses a serious threat to the integrity of the game. Widespread use by players of such substances unfairly disadvantages the honest athletes who refuse to use them and raises questions about the validity of baseball records."[8]

Mitchell's report spread the blame for steroid use around to everyone connected with baseball: the players and their labor

Former U.S. senator George Mitchell, with members of his investigating committee, speaks to the media in 2007 about his report on the use of performance-enhancing drugs in Major League Baseball.

union, the Major League Players Association; the Commissioner, and club officials. He asserted that no one recognized the problem steroids presented until it had become firmly entrenched, and by that time, steroid abuse was widespread. He urged baseball officials to investigate more thoroughly allegations of steroid use; develop a comprehensive education program for players about the health risks of steroids and performance-enhancing drugs; and incorporate year-round, random, unannounced drug testing. Mitchell concluded that the first step to gaining a sport without steroids and performance-enhancing substances is to adopt these recommendations.

A Short History of the Use of Steroids in Sports

Steroids are hormones that are naturally produced by the body. Male hormones are anabolic and androgenic. Anabolic steroids build up tissues, particularly muscles, bones, and red blood cells; androgenic steroids develop male sexual characteristics, such as body hair, a deep voice, and aggressiveness. Both anabolic and androgenic steroids are usually referred to as just "steroids." Testosterone is an anabolic androgenic steroid that was isolated by scientists in the 1930s. Once testosterone was isolated, it was relatively easy for scientists to find other steroids and synthesize them in the laboratory.

Medical Uses

Scientists and doctors were excited about the development of synthetic steroids because they could use them to treat myriad diseases and disorders. Because the effects of anabolic steroids are to build up muscles and bones, help bodies recover faster, increase the production of red blood cells, and increase feelings of well-being and energy, the Allies found them to be a great help in treating the starving prisoners in the Nazi concentration camps at the end of World War II. Anabolic steroids are also effective at treating people who suffer from chronic wasting disease due to AIDS or cancer. Jesse Haggard, a naturopathic doctor and author of the book *Demystifying Steroids*, writes that he prescribed steroids for a middle-aged patient who was wasting away due to a lack of appetite associated with the human immunodeficiency

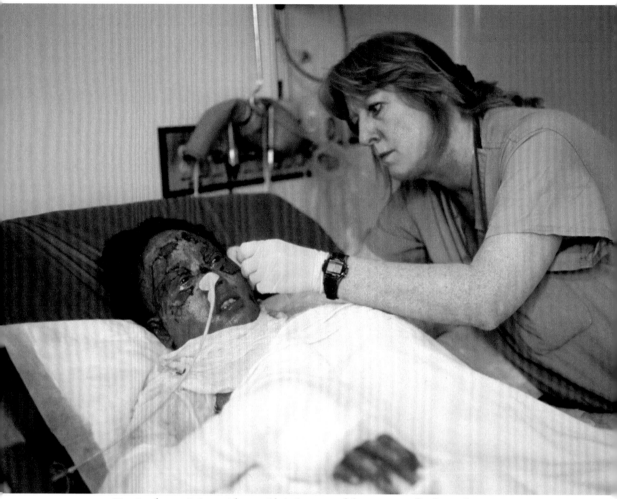

Treating burn victims with steroids is just one of the many medical uses for steroids.

virus. After four weeks on steroids, the patient gained 15 pounds (6.8kg) and "looked fantastically healthy."[9]

Because steroids are well known for stimulating muscle and tissue growth, they are also used to treat burn victims. For some unknown reason, testosterone production stops in people with severe burns. A study at the Shriners Burns Hospital at the University of Texas in Galveston found that burn patients who were injected with testosterone gained more muscle mass than burn patients who did not receive testosterone injections. Arny Ferrando, a researcher on the study, said, "I would say within two to three weeks that it's fairly noticeable that they start putting on weight."[10] Furthermore, he added, the burn patients using steroids gained lean muscle mass, whereas the burn patients who did not use steroids gained fat, not muscles. Moreover, the burn patients on steroids reported greater gains in strength.

Steroids are used to stimulate bone marrow production as well. In a rare but extremely serious condition called Diamond Blackfan anemia, the bone marrow does not produce enough red blood cells. Red blood cells carry oxygen to the tissues in the body; a lack of oxygen will cause the tissue to die. In one study a large group of people with Diamond Blackfan anemia were given steroids to stimulate their bone marrow into producing red blood cells. It was a very successful treatment; the bone marrow in 82 percent of the people responded to this treatment and began producing red blood cells.

Human growth hormone (hGH) is another steroid that has been successfully used to treat medical conditions such as children's growth disorders and hGH deficiencies in adults. Growth hormone is an anabolic steroid that is produced in the pituitary gland. Children who have a deficiency of hGH grow noticeably slower than other children, and if not treated, they will be shorter than average, have poor bone and muscle development, have an immature face, may experience hypoglycemia (low blood sugar), and may be chubby. Adults with growth hormone deficiency have decreased muscle and bone density, low energy, and are often obese. Treatment of children or adults with growth hormone deficiencies consists of raising the hGH levels to normal. Growth hormone given to children prior to puberty can accelerate their rate of growth and increase muscle development. Growth hormone given after puberty will not have an effect on height, since the bones have stopped growing. In adults hGH builds muscles, increases energy, and reduces body fat.

Weight Lifters Discover Steroids

Because of the effects that steroids have on the body—building up muscles and increasing red blood cells—trainers, coaches, and athletes started using the drugs as early as the 1950s in their training programs. Athletes found that if they took steroids, they were able to train harder, they developed more muscle mass and body strength, and they increased their energy levels, all beyond what they would be able to accomplish without steroids.

The first documented use of steroids in athletic competition was during the 1952 Olympic Games in Helsinki, Finland. Weight lifters from the Soviet Union won seven medals, including three golds. The U.S. weight lifting coach, Bob Hoffman, told reporters, "I know they're taking the hormone stuff to increase their strength."[11] A Soviet team physician confirmed Hoffman's suspicions two years later. The coach confessed to an American team physician, John Ziegler, at the World Weightlifting Championships in 1954, where the Soviets continued their domination of weight lifting.

HUMAN GROWTH HORMONE IS NOT DANGEROUS

"There is no published literature showing that hGH has caused any permanent side effects, or death. It's one of the best-researched drugs out there. The critics shouldn't make [danger] proclamations without a scientific basis. Show me the studies that say these treatments cause cancer or diabetes."—Ronald M. Klatz, the founder of the American Academy of Anti-Aging Medicine, a new medical specialty, on the benefits of human growth hormone.

Quoted in Arlene Weintraub, "The Guru of Anti-aging," *BusinessWeek Online*, March 20, 2006. www.businessweek.com/magazine/content/06_12/b3976009.htm.

Experimenting on himself and others, Ziegler, who worked at a pharmaceutical company, developed an oral synthetic steroid that replicated many of testosterone's muscle-building properties while reducing its negative side effects, such as aggressiveness, increased libido, risk of prostate problems, and hairiness. The result was Dianabol, which was to have been used on burn patients, but was quickly adopted by Hoffman and members of his bodybuilding club in York, Pennsylvania.

The first documented use of steroids in sports was at the 1952 Olympics. Soviet weight lifters used hormones to increase their strength.

The results were dramatic; the bodybuilders quickly bulked up while using the little pink pills. Hoffman tried to keep his bodybuilders' use of Dianabol a secret, claiming their impressive weight gains and beefy muscles were from a new training program he developed called isometric contraction. However, other bodybuilders were not able to duplicate the remarkable results—until they, too, discovered the secret to becoming muscular and strong was taking 5-milligram tablets of Dianabol. By the 1960s steroid use was commonplace among weight lifters and bodybuilders. Terry Todd, an elite weight lifter who took Dianabol during the 1960s, proved to his satisfaction that steroids worked. "Steroids," he said, "combined with proper training and nutrition, are able to produce athletic benefits, at least in the short run."[12]

Steroids at the Olympics

Soon athletes around the world began incorporating steroids into their training programs. In 1968 East Germany competed for the first time with its own teams of athletes at the Summer Olympic Games in Mexico City. East Germans won a total of twenty-five medals, including nine gold. Four years later in Munich, East Germany more than doubled its medal count with sixty-six medals, including twenty gold, coming in third behind the Soviet Union and the United States. According to Richard Pound, a member of the International Olympic Committee (IOC) and founder of the World Anti-Doping Agency (WADA), "By the time of the Montreal Games in 1976, the question in women's swimming was not how many gold medals the East Germans would win, but whether anyone else could win any."[13] His question was not far off the mark; East German women won ten gold medals in twelve events in women's swimming, and the East Germans again doubled the total number of gold medals they won: forty gold, along with fifty silver and bronze, second only to the Soviet Union in total medal count.

Sports for the Glory of the State

The Olympic Games were opened up to countries of the Eastern bloc in the 1960s to send individual teams to compete in the games. East Germany took this as an opportunity to show the world that the Communist system was responsible for the success of its athletes. East German women started dominating swimming competitions, including the Olympic Games, beginning in 1968. Due to the remarkable surge in the women's swim times and number of wins, steroids were suspected to be a part of the athletes' training program. Since no tests had yet been designed to detect the presence of steroids, nothing could be proved. Years later, though, an East German coach confirmed the rumors that the women swimmers were using steroids to American coach Sherm Chavoor, who had coached Mark Spitz to his seven gold medals during the 1972 Olympics in Munich. Chavoor said the coach asked him about American athletes and drugs, by "'point[ing] to his arm, like he had a needle in his other hand.' . . . Chavoor . . . said he told the coach that none of his swimmers used drugs, that drugs might be dangerous. He recalled the coach acting surprised and saying, 'But bodies are expendable.'"

Michael Janofsky, "Coaches Concede That Steroids Fueled East Germany's Success in Swimming," *New York Times*, December 3, 1991.

HGH QUACKERY

"Claims that human growth hormone and substances that stimulate its production work to stop or reverse aging or build strength are unfounded and the marketing of these substances for such purposes constitutes quackery and hucksterism. On the other side of the coin are the risks of arthritis, diabetes and cancer, and actually lower life expectancy."—Tom Perls, founder of the New England Centenarian Study, which researches why some people live to be one hundred years old or more.

Tom Perls, "The Real Truth About Growth Hormone for Anti-aging and Sports. It's Quackery and Hucksterism," Growth Hormone/HGH/Antiaging and Sports, June 18, 2008. http://hghwatch.com.

By this time it was suspected that East German athletes, especially the women swimmers, were doing something besides training to achieve such dramatic results. When a rival coach noted that the East German women swimmers had very deep voices, a telltale sign of steroid use in women, an East German coach responded, "We came here to swim, not sing."[14] While officials suspected the East Germans of doping their athletes, at the time there were no tests that could definitively prove the athletes were taking steroids, despite the fact that the IOC had begun testing athletes for drugs in 1968.

Steroids in Other Sports

Athletes who used steroids had taken over in weight lifting, bodybuilding, and swimming, and soon it seemed as though steroids had found their place in every sport. Athletes who used steroids were winning more competitions than those who stayed clean. Charlie Francis, a coach for Olympic track and field stars, told a Canadian government commission in 1989 that he was convinced that all the top track and field athletes were taking steroids. "I couldn't find a single case where it appeared that performance-enhancing drugs were not being used,"[15] he testified. Francis said he had been giving his athletes performance-enhancing substances for almost a decade because they had to

Some observers said that about two-thirds of the athletes at the 1972 Olympics were using performance-enhancing drugs.

"break the rules or lose."[16] Charles Yesalis, an expert in performance-enhancing drugs, claims that two-thirds of the athletes at the 1972 Olympics had used steroids at one time. According to Yesalis, the popular belief that athletes who take steroids "are only a few bad apples in the barrel" is false. In actuality, he said, "There's only a few good apples in the barrel."[17]

Adam Nelson, who won the silver medal in the shot put at the Olympics in Athens in 2004, claims to be one of those good apples. He is upset that everyone assumes that because he is good at his sport that he must be using drugs. "There's just a massive amount of misinformation that says the only way to improve performance substantially is through taking performance-enhancing drugs. . . . It used to frustrate the heck out of me—you can't throw this far or run this time or jump this far unless you do this."[18]

Football and Steroids

Steroid use in professional football was first documented in 1962–1963, and according to the National Football League's (NFL) former drug adviser Forrest Tennant, "athletes openly took them,"[19] at least until steroids were banned by the NFL in 1983. A 2008 report by the *San Diego Union-Tribune*, in which 185 NFL players are

The Elixir of Life

One of the first scientists to hypothesize about the existence of hormones was Charles-Édouard Brown-Séquard (1817–1894), who theorized that testicles produced an especially potent substance that had an immense impact on quality of life. Brown-Séquard made up a mixture of testicular blood, semen, and the "juice" from crushed dog or guinea pig testicles. He injected himself with this mixture ten times during a month-long period in 1889 when he was seventy-two years old. In an account of his self-experiment, he wrote that he had become weak and exhausted after working for just a few hours. But after several injections, he felt rejuvenated. He wrote of one example of the changes he noticed after the injection of his elixir:

From a natural impetuosity, and also to avoid losing time, I had, till I was sixty years old, the habit of ascending and descending stairs so rapidly that my movements were rather those of running than of walk. This had gradually changed, and I had come to move slowly up and down stairs, having to hold the banister in difficult staircases. After the second injection I found that I had fully regained my old powers, and returned to my previous habits in that respect.

C.E. Brown-Séquard, *The Elixir of Life*, ed. Newell Dunbar. Boston: J.G. Cupples, 1889, p. 29.

named as having taken performance-enhancing drugs, is not even considered to be a comprehensive list of players who used such drugs. "It is believed to only scratch the surface of actual usage in pro football,"[20] the paper asserts. Yesalis maintains that the names listed in the report are just "the tip of the iceberg."[21] The report claimed that entire football teams used steroids in the 1960s and 1970s and that the actual number of players who used steroids and other performance-enhancing drugs could number in the thousands, of which only a very tiny percentage were ever caught.

Cycling

Like football teams of the 1960s and 1970s, entire teams of professional cyclists have been caught using steroids and other performance-enhancing substances during major races, notably the Tour de France. The 2006 Tour de France was plagued with doping scandals. Favored cyclists Jan Ullrich of Germany and Ivan Basso of Italy were expelled from the race after their names were linked to Eufemiano Fuentes, a Spanish doctor who was accused of administering banned substances to more than two hundred athletes. In addition, two Spanish cycling teams were forced to withdraw from the race due to their involvement with Fuentes. American Floyd Landis had his win stripped from him after a drug test found abnormal levels of testosterone in his system. The 2007 Tour de France was practically a repeat of the year before; five cyclists and two teams were dismissed or withdrew from the race for failing drug tests. Greg LeMond, an American who won the Tour de France three times in the 1980s, said that performance-enhancing substances give the cyclist an unfair advantage. "Doping increases a cyclist's capacity 30 percent. At the top form of my career, I could not have finished in the leading 15 in the Tour today [because of the use of steroids in the sport],"[22] he told a French newspaper in 2007. In 2008 nine members of the Portuguese cycling team were suspended after officials found banned substances and doping equipment in the team's headquarters.

Baseball

Major League Baseball (MLB) was one of the last professional sport organizations to ban performance-enhancing drugs. Ken

Floyd Landis, the winner of the 2006 Tour de France, was stripped of his title for using performance-enhancing drugs.

Caminiti, who was named the National League's Most Valuable Player in 1996, admitted to *Sports Illustrated* that he was a heavy user of steroids during his MVP year. He told the magazine that steroid use was common in baseball: "It's no secret what's going on in baseball. At least half the guys are using steroids. They talk about it. They joke about it with each other."[23] Jose Canseco, who played baseball for sixteen years in the major leagues, wrote in his book *Juiced* that the majority of ballplayers used steroids: "If I had to guess, I'd say eight out of every ten players had kits in their lockers filled with growth hormones, steroids, supplements—you name it."[24] According to Canseco, some of the greatest baseball players of the 1990s and first decade of the 2000s used steroids: Mark McGwire, Barry Bonds, Sammy Sosa, Miguel Tejada, Jason Giambi, and Rafael Palmeiro, among others.

Since the publication of Canseco's book, Major League Baseball commissioned a report, conducted by former senator George

In Jose Canseco's 2005 book, Juiced, *the former MVP made the accusation that "at least half the guys [in Major League Baseball] are using steroids."*

J. Mitchell, to investigate steroid use in baseball. The Mitchell report named eighty-five baseball players who admitted to, or were accused by other players of, using steroids. Since the report's release in 2007, numerous players have been named as using steroids. MLB started cracking down on players who tested positive for steroids. In May 2009 it suspended Manny Ramirez of the Los Angles Dodgers for fifty games when he tested positive for human chorionic gonadotropin, a banned performance enhancer that is used to stimulate testosterone production after finishing a cycle of steroid drugs.

TESTOSTERONE IS LINKED TO PROSTATE CANCER

"We know for a fact that testosterone and related steroids can accelerate the growth of prostate cancer, sometimes causing a tiny island of cancerous cells in the prostate to progress to full-blown, aggressively spreading disease."—Harrison G. Pope Jr., Katharine A. Phillips, and Roberto Olivardia, authors of *The Adonis Complex: The Secret Crisis of Male Body Obsession*, on the link between testosterone and prostate cancer.

Harrison G. Pope Jr., Katharine A. Phillips, Roberto Olivardia, *The Adonis Complex: The Secret Crisis of Male Body Obsession*. New York: Free Press, 2000, p. 118.

Steroid Numbers in Teens

The 2008 Monitoring the Future survey had encouraging news about teens and steroids. Steroid use among eighth, tenth, and twelfth graders had decreased or held steady for the past decade. According to the survey, only 1.4 percent of eighth and tenth graders had ever used steroids, and 2.2 percent of twelfth graders had used steroids. However, the Centers for Disease Control's 2007 Youth Risk Behavior Survey found that 3.9 percent of ninth through twelfth graders had used steroids at least once in their lives, although that percentage had fallen from a high of 6.1 percent in 2003. Between the two surveys, approximately three hundred thousand to five hundred thousand teens have used steroids.

THE STEROIDS MYTH

"Most people are familiar with the idea that steroids cause prostate cancer. However, it has never been proven in medical research. The belief that steroids are 'fuel for fire' in regard to prostate cancer is a myth. Steroids use does not cause cancer. The fact is, the opposite has been proven."—Jesse Haggard, a naturopathic doctor who wrote a book about the benefits of steroids.

Jesse Haggard, *Demystifying Steroids*. Bloomington, IN: AuthorHouse, 2008, p. 51.

Like other surveys of steroid use, accurate counts of college athletes who use steroids and other performance-enhancing drugs are notoriously hard to get. One early study found that 20 percent of college athletes had used steroids by 1984, but according to the National Collegiate Athletic Association (NCAA), steroid use has fallen dramatically since then. Drug tests and penalties for positive results seem to have a deterrent effect on steroid use. Drug tests reveal that the number of college athletes who have tested positive for banned substances has fallen to 3 percent. In 1986 the NCAA started testing college athletes for drugs and steroids before championship games. When Brian Bosworth, a linebacker for the University of Oklahoma, and two of his teammates tested positive for steroids that year, the NCAA ruled they were ineligible to play in the Orange Bowl.

Still Readily Available

Despite state and federal laws restricting steroids, athletes who really want them can usually find a source easily. Steroids are still legal with or without a prescription in many other countries, most notably Mexico, Thailand, and many European countries. Moreover, numerous Web sites sell steroids online, although many of the steroids are counterfeit or fake. Like adults, most teens have no problem buying steroids over the Internet. "It was a frigging piece of cake," said Joe P., a teen in south Florida. "I had the [steroids] delivered right to my parents' house."[25] Steroids are often sold on the black market at gyms, competitions, and sometimes from coaches and trainers, and occasionally from doctors, pharmacists, and veterinarians. (Steroids used for animals are often the same or similar to those used on humans.) For those who are chemically inclined, the raw ingredients may be purchased and combined to produce homemade versions of anabolic steroids.

Steroids bought in foreign countries, on the black market, or from veterinarians present even more dangers to users than the potential adverse side effects. These drugs are often not made with the same degree of quality control, and they are sometimes produced in unsterile and unsanitary environments.

WHY USE STEROIDS?

Adult men make up the majority of steroid users, followed by women, with just a small percentage of teens who take steroids. The number of teens using steroids has been steadily declining since 2003; about 2.2 percent of twelfth graders in the 2007 Monitoring the Future study admitted using steroids, which is down from an all-time high of 4 percent in 2003. Robert Voy, a former chief medical officer for the U.S. Olympic Committee, estimates that the number of high school students using steroids is even higher: "One in six high school players use steroids to compete."[26]

While many of the side effects given for taking steroids may or may not appear in adult men, the side effects are much more likely to occur in children and women. And therein lies the problem, according to Nathan Jendrick, author of *Dunks, Doubles, Doping: How Steroids Are Killing American Athletics*. Jendrick writes: "Most kids probably don't go to bed wondering what a cycle of Anadrol would do to them, but imagining what it would feel like to be a starting pitcher for the Yankees is as common as sunshine."[27]

Steroid Abuse

Steroids are drugs that must be prescribed by a doctor. Like other drugs, they have positive and negative effects on the body. Taken properly and under a doctor's orders, low doses of steroid drugs reduce inflammation and provide pain relief due to arthritis, bursitis, and tendonitis; stimulate appetites; and help build up muscles and other tissues that have wasted away due to muscle-wasting diseases such as cancer or AIDS. However, athletes who use steroids to help them build up muscles use doses that are higher than recommended, and these dosages can cause dangerous and irreversible side effects.

Steroids are usually taken either orally, in pill form, or injected. Athletes tend to take several different types of steroids at the same time, in a process called stacking. For example, one steroid is used as the base to build muscle mass, another steroid may be used to promote tissue and muscle recovery after workouts, and a third

Steroids are usually taken orally, in pill form, or injected.

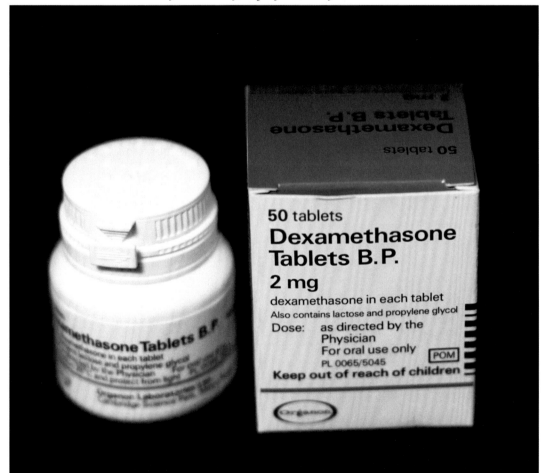

steroid may be used to increase body strength. Athletes typically start with a low dose of steroids, building up the dosage over a period of several weeks. Then these athletes begin a period of reducing the dosages, while adding other steroids and supplements. This process of taking increasing and decreasing dosages of steroids is called cycling. An entire cycle may last twelve to eighteen weeks. During a cycle, or in between cycles, athletes often forgo taking steroids for a couple of weeks. Some steroids are effective for only a few weeks at a time; some steroids are toxic to the liver or other organs when taken long term; and some steroids may stop the body from being able to produce testosterone or may cause it to produce an excess of the female hormone estrogen. It is during these down times that athletes will take other supplements to help the body recover from the steroids and help it start producing its own hormones again. Then after a few weeks off, the athlete starts the cycle all over again.

Steroids and Sports

Those with dreams of becoming the next athletic superstar—whether in high school, college, the pros, or the Olympics—may begin taking steroids because they want to be the best athlete in their sport. Jendrick, a personal trainer and former competitor in amateur bodybuilding contests, writes:

> Olympic athletes often consider that representing their countries is an honor. Other professional athletes, while not representing their country, represent themselves and want simply to show the world they are the top athlete in their profession. Of course, with that comes big money, endorsement deals for products they don't always use, shoes named after them, and a slew of admirers. . . . not a bad deal, really.[28]

For many athletes, steroids do give them the boost they need to become the best in their sports. For example, several baseball records that stood unchallenged for decades were broken by players who either admitted to or are suspected of taking steroids.

Many athletes, even those in high school, use steroids because they think they need bigger muscles to be good enough to compete in sports. Dan Nieboer, a football, track, and power lifting coach at a Texas high school, warns his athletes about trying to bulk up. There are, he says, "muscles that work well for them as an athlete and muscles that look good. They don't necessarily go hand in hand." Bulging biceps, he continues, are "not necessarily going to make you a better basketball player or football player." Furthermore, he tells his student athletes that teen bodies are not meant to have bulging muscles. The bones and muscles in teenage bodies are still developing. "With the faster metabolism at the age of 15 or 16, you're not going to get huge. You will increase and get bigger gradually, but not until you're 22 or 23,"[29] he asserts. In addition, the bodies of teens and youth do not handle steroid use well while they are still developing. Steroids can cause the young body's growth plates to fuse together, resulting in a height that is shorter than it would have been without steroids.

STEROIDS BUILD MUSCLES AND INCREASE STRENGTH

"It has been proved that anabolic steroid use, combined with weight training and adequate dietary protein intake, can build muscle mass and strength over and above weight training alone."—William N. Taylor, author of *Anabolic Steroids and the Athlete*, Jefferson, NC: McFarland, 2002, p. 65.

Dan Clark, who played the gladiator Nitro on the television show *American Gladiator*, injured his knee playing football in his freshman year of junior college. During his rehabilitation after knee surgery, he dropped from 210 pounds (95kg) down to a scrawny 178 pounds (81kg). A friend at his gym told him about steroids and how they would help him get his strength back in a hurry. Clark saw a doctor who prescribed two steroids for him, Dianabol and testosterone cypionate. Warned about the side effects, Clark said he was more worried that the steroids would not work for him, a worry that turned out to be groundless. He says:

Many sports require long, lean muscles rather than the bulked-up, shortened muscles that steroids promote.

"The steroids don't just work, they are everything the doctor said they would be, and more. I'm surprised by how fast my body responds to the drugs. One day I'm benching 185, the next, 225. I get big, ripped, and strong, and I gain back all the weight I lost from surgery, plus an additional ten pounds."[30] Clark was elated by the changes in his body brought on by steroids, especially when he earned the Most Valuable Player award during his sophomore year and a scholarship to play football at a state college.

Steroids in Professional Sports

Steroids are perhaps used the most by athletes in professional sports, although nearly all professional sports organizations have instituted rules against steroid use by their players. Estimates for the number of professional athletes who use steroids vary widely. Former baseball player and admitted steroid user Jose Canseco believes that 80 percent or more of professional ballplayers use steroids, while Major League Baseball contends that steroids were used by only 5 to 7 percent of the players in the first decade of the 2000s. According to Canseco, "The challenge is not to find a top player who has used steroids. The challenge is to find a top

Steroids Enhance an Athlete's Natural Ability

Jose Canseco, a former Major League Baseball player and an admitted steroids user, writes in his book *Juiced: Wild Times, Rampant 'Roids, Smash Hits, and How Baseball Got Big*, that he was the "godfather" of steroids; he takes personal credit for introducing steroids to Major League Baseball players. He believes that steroids are responsible for transforming him—and many other baseball players—into superstars. He adds, however, that steroids will not make ballplayers superstars if they do not have talent:

> People always talk about how steroids can't give you hand-eye coordination, and in a sense, that's true. If you've got no natural ability, steroids aren't going to give it to you. But if you are naturally

athletic, steroids can enhance whatever you have, both in terms of strength and stamina, and also in terms of hand-eye coordination and performance. For example, I noticed that during the season, most athletes get tired. You start out great, but you lose 20 or 30 percent of your strength and bat speed. A player who started out hitting a lot of home runs would taper off toward the end, because he was just physically tired. Since I was new to it all, I didn't know that steroids could help you with that.

Jose Canseco, *Juiced: Wild Times, Rampant 'Roids, Smash Hits, and How Baseball Got Big*. New York: Regan, 2005, p. 50.

player who *hasn't*." Moreover, Canseco contends that most baseball players have thought about using steroids:

> Every single major-league player has at least given steroid use some thought, weighed the positives and negatives. How could you not? Ball players earn their living with their bodies, after all. They all want to become bigger, stronger, and faster. Of course, they'd be tempted to do anything they could to improve those bodies. . . . If you get bigger, stronger, and can hit more home runs, you can make a lot more money.[31]

According to Canseco, most players came around to his way of thinking and started using steroids to improve their performance. In fact, he says, baseball team owners and other high-ranking club officials are responsible for the surge in steroid use among their players because those in charge of the players' union "fought for years to make sure players wouldn't be tested for steroids." In addition, he says, club owners quietly "put the word out that they want home runs and excitement, . . . that whatever it is the players are doing to become superhuman, they sure ought to keep it up." Canseco argues that the public agrees with the owners. "People want to be entertained at the ballpark. They want baseball to be fun and exciting. Home runs are fun and exciting. . . . Steroid-enhanced athletes hit more home runs."[32]

STEROIDS ENHANCE ATHLETIC PERFORMANCE

"[Barry] Bonds, the superstar leftfielder for the San Francisco Giants, the six-time most valuable player, the man who obliterated the single-season home-run record, the hitter who is in the best position to pass Hank Aaron on the all-time home-run list, is putting up numbers at an age when most major leaguers are hitting golf balls, not baseballs."—Don Walker and Mark Maley, reporters for the *Milwaukee Journal Sentinel,* on how Bonds's performance on the field improved during a time in which he later admitted to taking steroids.

Don Walker and Mark Maley, "Bonds' Brilliance Has Asterisk," *Milwaukee Journal Sentinel,* March 28, 2004, p. C1.

Teens and Steroids

Because athletes are often considered role models who are idolized by teens and children, many people worry about the effect steroid use by athletes will have on youth. They fear that because athletes use steroids, teens will try to emulate their heroes and use steroids as well. According to Bernard Griesemer, an expert on steroid use in teen athletes, and the author of the American Academy of Pediatrics' position paper on steroids, "What athletes wear, do, say, and take have a huge impact on your young athletes."[33] That influence, he says, includes steroid use. If athletic superstars are using steroids, it is more likely that young athletes will emulate their heroes and use steroids, too.

SPORTS ARE UNFAIR

"Sports are inherently unfair. Genes alone do not make you a winner, of course, but some people's genes give them a massive advantage."—Michael LePage, a writer for the magazine *New Scientist*.

Michael LePage, "Only Drugs Can Stop the Sports Cheats," *New Scientist*, August 19, p. 206.

Peer Pressure and Other Influences

High school students are also more apt to use steroids as a result of peer pressure than older athletes. The number one reason students give for why they succumbed to peer pressure is that they did not want to appear different from their peers. Moreover, if other athletes are using steroids, some teens may feel they have to take steroids in order to be competitive.

Coaches also may influence athletes to take steroids—inadvertently or deliberately—by making comments about the athletes' body or size. "Comments such as 'You could stand to gain a few extra pounds,' or 'If you were bigger you could play on the team,' send a message,"[34] says Joseph Berning, an exercise physiologist and assistant professor at New Mexico State University. Some student athletes, especially those who feel pressure

The Media Advertises the Steroid Look to Teens

It is not just athletes who are hoping to gain strength and power that use steroids. Teens, specifically teen boys, are overwhelmed by images of muscular bodies, according to Linn Goldberg, the cofounder of ATLAS and ATHENA, two programs that educate teen athletes about proper nutrition and the dangers of steroid use. He testified before Congress about how the media shapes teens' ideas about their bodies, saying:

The media influences teens. Over the past ten years, hyper-muscular pictures are frequently on the cover of many magazines. Children's items and images from GI Joe figures to comic strip characters have had a "steroidal" makeover, reflecting unrealistic muscular body types. The advertising tactic using the term "on steroids" is often used to market products that include automobiles, software, negotiating seminars, notepads and running shoes. This strategy suggests that their product is so superb, it is similar to being on steroids.

Linn Goldberg, Testimony Before the U.S. House of Representatives, Committee on Government Reform, April 27, 2005. http://oversight.house.gov/documents/20050 427111957-63760.pdf.

Linn Goldberg, cofounder of the antisteroid programs ATLAS and ATHENA, argues that advertisers target teens and promote the "steroid look."

to perform well so that they will be selected to play a sport for college or professional teams, may feel pressure to use steroids to get big and strong fast. The lure of lucrative contracts and salaries encourages some to use steroids to enhance their records and statistics. Kris Castellanos, a baseball player for Florida State University, explained why many college athletes decide to use steroids. "Guys are thinking that's pretty much the only way to get there or that's the easiest way to get where they want to."[35]

High school students also take steroids to look good for the opposite sex, rather than trying to bulk up for a sport. Dionne Roberts was seventeen years old and a high school cheerleader and gymnast. She wanted to look toned, to have that look of "six-pack abs,"[36] as she described it, and so she started taking steroids. She says: "It's not uncommon to strive for that four-pack or six-pack, even in girls. Being in shape is not just a masculine thing." She said she was influenced to use steroids by the images she saw on television and in the movies. "It's this whole Hollywood thing," she said. "Everyone is so affected by movie stars and that whole pop culture thing. I think it takes over a little bit. We have to get back to reality. Everybody has their own quarrels with self-esteem and self-image, and that's what every young woman goes through."[37]

An Attempt to Look Good

Teens are not the only ones who use steroids in order to improve their image or who want to bulk up and get bigger. Personal trainers, models, dancers, and even movie stars, as well as some firefighters, police officers, and military service members use steroids because they want to change their body image by bulking up or developing their muscles. Some may want to change their bodies because they want to perform better in their chosen sport or profession, while others just want to look fit and muscular. Adolescents and teens often become preoccupied with their body and body image. Insecurities about fitting in with their peers and looking desirable to members of the opposite sex may lead some teens to try steroids. One young man said he bought some steroid pills at his gym to look better for women:

I was always kind of skinny, and thought that I could go on a small cycle and get a bit bigger, and be more attractive to women. I bought some pink pills from a guy at my gym. I think they were called "Diana-ball" [Dianabol]. I thought that was great, because I was trying to meet more girls, and "Diana" is a girl's name. . . . Before I knew it, my hairline started getting higher and the hair on the back of my head started getting thinner. I was going bald in my early 20's! I stopped using the little pink pills, but it didn't matter. The hair never really grew back, even after I stopped.[38]

Like many steroid users, this young man thought of just the end results he wanted without ever considering the possible side effects from taking the steroids.

Side Effects

Athletes have to deal with many side effects from steroids. Not all users develop all these side effects, nor do they necessarily develop side effects to the extent listed here. Nevertheless, side effects are a real concern to users.

Changes to the skin are a typical sign of steroid abuse. Androgenic steroids (steroids that develop and promote masculine traits and characteristics) stimulate the sebaceous glands, which secrete oils in the skin. The excessive secretion of oils can cause rampant acne on the back, shoulders and chest, and occasionally on the face. While dermatologists may be able to prescribe ointments to treat the acne, many of the scars and changes to the skin from acne are permanent.

Some steroids also contribute to the development of gynecomastia, or the development of breasts in men. The body has an enzyme called aromatase that converts excess testosterone from steroids into estrogen, the female hormone, and estrogen is responsible for developing breast tissue. In addition, an excess of estrogen will stop the production of testosterone, which will lead to shriveled and shrunken testicles. Clark writes in his tell-all book *Gladiator* about the side effects he suffered from using steroids:

Steroids that develop masculine traits and characteristics also stimulate the sebaceous glands, which leads to acne.

As a result of twenty years of steroid use, I walk with a limp, I have seven scars on my face, two destroyed knees, and I can't walk up a flight of stairs until I chug a couple of cups of black coffee and a handful of anti-inflammatory pills. What strapping eighteen-year-old athlete could ever imagine ending up with a herniated back disk and a neck that pops like fireworks on the Fourth of July from a mere turn of my head? And those are the obvious problems. The *real* prizes are a pair of shrunken testicles and surgical scars across my nipples from having breast tissue removed from my chest.[39]

These are the side effects that no one wants to hear about, Clark writes.

FASTER RECOVERY FROM WORKOUTS

"By far, the biggest effect of THG [was] enhanced recovery. It didn't make me bigger or faster or stronger, necessarily. It made me less stiff and sore after my strenuous workouts, helped me recover from workouts, and reduced soreness, enabling me to work at a higher level longer. . . . It gave me an edge that my diet, sleep, and endless training sessions could no longer provide."—Bill Romanowski, former football player with the Oakland Raiders, on why he took the performance-enhancing substance the Clear, also known as THG.

Bill Romanowski with Adam Shefter and Phil Towle, *Romo: My Life on the Edge: Living Dreams and Slaying Dragons*. New York: HarperCollins, 2005, p. 222.

Organ Damage

Perhaps three of the most serious of the side effects involve the liver, kidneys, and prostate gland. The prolonged use of some steroids has been shown to cause severe liver damage and development of blood-filled cysts on the liver and has been linked to liver cancer. Steroid use is also linked to kidney tumors, and, especially if the athlete has high blood pressure, kidney damage. The use of testosterone is linked to an enlarged prostate, which often precedes prostate cancer.

The prolonged use of steroids can cause cancer in the liver like the one pictured here.

'Roid Rage

Playing with the levels of hormones in the body can also cause depression and mood swings. In addition, high testosterone levels are linked to aggressiveness. An athlete who increases his testosterone level through steroids is also increasing his feelings of aggression. While increased aggressiveness allows some athletes to train harder and longer, others cannot cope with their feelings and become easily irritated, impatient, and prone to angry outbursts. These symptoms are referred to as 'roid rage. Some athletes and bodybuilders are suspected of killing their family members and themselves during periods of 'roid rage caused by steroid use.

Side Effects in Women

Steroid use is not confined strictly to men. The number of women athletes who use steroids has also grown dramatically, especially during the past few years. Side effects from using steroids—many of which are androgenic, or muscle builders—affect men and women differently. In addition, many of the side effects that are temporary in men are irreversible in women. Gynecomastia in men may take more than one cycle to appear, and will usually disappear (or at least diminish) when the male athlete discontinues steroid use. The changes in women, however, often occur during their first cycle of steroid use. When on steroids, a woman's voice deepens, facial hair increases, and a woman's clitoris enlarges, often to a size of two to three inches. (The clitoris is the organ responsible for the woman's sexual pleasure.) While an enlarged clitoris will shrink slightly when the woman stops taking steroids, it will not go back to its normal size. Nor will a woman's voice that has changed due to steroid use change back to a more feminine register.

Birth Defects

Because steroids are synthetic sex hormones, women who take steroids are at risk of permanently damaging their reproductive systems. Their menstrual cycles may slow or even stop, and the steroids may even make them infertile. Unlike men, women's infertility due to steroid abuse can often be permanent. More importantly, a woman who takes steroids while pregnant is risking the health of her unborn child. The abnormally high levels of steroids in a woman's body during pregnancy can cause mental retardation or the development of both male and female sexual organs (called hermaphroditism) in her fetus.

A study of fifty-two Olympic athletes from East Germany—who were told the steroids they were systematically given by their trainers during the 1960s and 1970s were vitamins—found that their children had a much higher rate of serious medical issues than the general population. The athletes lost fifteen children due to miscarriage, and three were stillborn, a rate thirty-two times higher than the normal German population. Giselher Spitzer, the study's author, found that of the sixty-nine children who survived, seven were physically handicapped, four were mentally handicapped, 25 percent had allergies, and 23 percent had asthma. "Children of mothers who were drugged typically suffer more from multiple handicaps than children of drugged fathers," Spitzer said at a 2007 conference on sport and society, and added, "54 percent of the children suffer from two illnesses."[40] He concluded that taking steroids is dangerous for everyone involved. "Your children will be damaged by that practice, and many athletes . . . say 'It is my body and I'll do what I want.' It is not the truth, it's not only your body, it is the second generation, and we don't know what will be of the third generation."[41]

There are many reasons why people take steroids. Used properly, steroids will build muscles, increase muscle strength, and speed recovery time after workouts. Few users are completely educated about how to use steroids properly, however, and so they risk experiencing dangerous side effects from the steroids. Scientists and health professionals still do not know all the effects long-term steroid use have on the body.

Is It Cheating to Use Steroids?

Some of the biggest stars in baseball have—or soon might have—an asterisk (*) placed beside their statistics in the record books. The asterisk, as one sportswriter wrote, "howls that the marked achievement emits a whiff of the tainted."[42] When Roger Maris hit his sixty-first home run, surpassing Babe Ruth's record of sixty homers in a season, Baseball Commissioner Ford Frick placed an asterisk by the number 61 because Maris played in 162 games, compared to Ruth's 154. (The asterisk was later removed.) The baseball Barry Bonds hit out of the park in 2007 for his 756th career home run, surpassing Hank Aaron's record of 755, was branded with an asterisk before it was placed in the Baseball Hall of Fame in Cooperstown, New York. The asterisk, according to the ball's owner who placed it on the ball, suggests that Bonds cheated in achieving his home run record because he took steroids.

Tainted by Steroids

Some sportswriters and baseball fans cheered at the news of the asterisk. They believe that all players who take steroids should have asterisks next to their numbers. Michael Wilbon, a sportswriter with the *Washington Post*, maintains that the forty-three-year-old, arthritic Bonds has a tarnished record that deserves an asterisk. "It's fair to put an asterisk next to Bonds's totals, perhaps even necessary, because he has arthritic knees . . . and without steroid-driven workouts, it's reasonable to presume he wouldn't be physically able to play anymore. . . . Without steroids, it's fair to think Bonds would have had to retire a year

Many people feel that Barry Bonds's record-breaking 756th career home run ball should be marked with an asterisk because of Bonds's alleged steroid use.

or two ago, maybe at 660 home runs."[43] These same sportswriters and fans believe that Sammy Sosa, Mark McGwire, Jose Canseco, and other athletes who took steroids deserve asterisks as well.

Not everyone believes athletes who take steroids have tainted sports records, however. Canseco, an admitted steroid user, asserts that steroids are good for the game of baseball. He predicts that

A Huge Trust

A common excuse heard from athletes who are accused of doping is that they were taking supplements given to them by their coach or trainer without knowing what they were taking. Many athletes and their coaches ordered legal supplements and—if they had the right connections—illegal performance-enhancing steroids from the Bay Area Laboratory Co-Op (BALCO) in the San Francisco area. A grand jury called baseball player Barry Bonds to testify about BALCO and his personal steroid use. Bonds claimed they were not steroids but supplements and that he never asked his trainer about them. "When he said it was flaxseed oil, I just said, 'Whatever.' It was in the ballpark . . . in front of everybody. I mean, all the reporters, my teammates. I mean, they all saw it. I didn't hide it. I didn't hide it. . . .

You know, trainers come up to me and say, 'Hey Barry, try this.'" Then Bonds was asked if his trainer "came to you at the ballpark with some other substance, whatever it is, if he asked you to take some other substance and said it was some other type of oil, whatever he asked you to take, would you take it?" Bonds answered, "I would trust that he wouldn't do anything to hurt me." The prosecutor pressed Bonds on this issue, asking him again, "Okay. But you wouldn't ask any further questions. You'd just basically—because he's your friend, if he asked you to take it, you would take it?" Bonds replied, "He would do the same thing for me."

Barry Bonds, 2003 Grand Jury Testimony, December 4, 2003. http://mlb.mlb.com/mlb/news/bonds030208.pdf.

Barry Bonds leaves the federal building where he testified before a grand jury in the Bay Area Laboratory Co-Operative (BALCO) investigation into drug violations.

someday, "every baseball player and pro athlete will be using at least low levels of steroids. As a result, baseball and other sports will be more exciting and entertaining."[44] Many fans seem to agree that steroids make sports more exciting. While Canseco, Bonds, and Alex Rodriguez all were heckled by fans in the stands for using steroids, sportswriter Wilbon says that he sees few signs of outrage from fans about steroid use. Most fans who respond to his news stories and columns on steroid use by athletes seem indifferent, he writes. "For every e-mail expressing true outrage, . . . there are five from fans who either still don't know exactly what to feel or are more hurt or annoyed than angry."[45] Athletes say they are taking steroids for these fans; they are just giving people what they want—a more exciting and entertaining game.

An Unfair Advantage

Athletes who admit to using steroids say they do so because they want the bigger muscles, the extra strength, the greater endurance, and the faster recovery time after working out that steroids give them. Ken Caminiti, one of the first Major League Baseball players to admit to using steroids, said that athletes who use steroids do not consider the drug use to be cheating because the drugs simply allow them to live up to their potential. Baseball, he said, is "still a hand-eye coordination game, but the difference [with steroids] is the ball is going to go a little farther. Some of the balls that would go to the warning track will go out. That's the difference."[46]

STEROIDS HAVE NO PLACE IN SPORT

"Doping is cheating and, in many cases, dangerous cheating. It has no place in sport. The sport rules must be applied to protect the overwhelming majority of athletes who play fairly. Cheaters cannot be allowed to go on cheating."—Richard Pound, founder of the World Anti-Doping Agency, the organization that tests Olympic and other athletes for signs of steroid use.

Richard Pound, *Inside Dope: How Drugs Are the Biggest Threat to Sports, Why You Should Care, and What Can Be Done About Them*. Mississaugua, ON: Wiley, p. 15.

Caminiti and others assert that while steroids may enhance an athlete's natural abilities, such as running, lifting weights, and throwing balls, the athlete still has to have the ability to do these things well in the first place. According to Bonds, using steroids is absolutely immaterial to how well an athlete plays. "In baseball it really doesn't matter what you do; you still have to hit that base-ball," he told reporters after hitting a two-run home run. "If you're incapable of hitting it, it doesn't matter what you take. You have to have eye-hand coordination to be able to produce. I think [steroid use] is really irrelevant to the game of baseball."[47]

ERASED FROM THE RECORD BOOKS

"If you get caught using steroids, you should have everything you've done in this game wiped out for any period of time that you used it. A lot of players, I think, have said as much because it is cheating."—Curt Schilling, former pitcher with the Boston Red Sox, discussing Barry Bonds's achievements during a period in which he later admitted using steroids.

Quoted in Steve Silva, "Curt on Bonds," Boston.com, May 8, 2007. www.boston.com/sports/baseball/redsox/extras/extra_bases/2007/05/curt_on_bonds_1.html.

In addition, these athletes must go through a rigorous train-ing schedule to take advantage of the benefits bestowed by steroids. One of the primary benefits of using steroids is that they build muscles. When athletes work out while taking steroids, the steroids help the muscles become bigger than they would have been without the steroids. Athletes also develop greater en-durance and speed due to the steroids' muscle-building effects than if they had worked out without using steroids. Another very important aspect of steroid usage is that they help athletes' mus-cles recover from a workout faster. All these benefits allow an ath-lete to train harder and for longer periods of time, which results in greater gains in strength, endurance, and speed than would otherwise be possible. Perhaps most importantly, these key ben-efits disappear if the athlete stops taking steroids or working out.

Steroid use can give athletes greater endurance and speed and help muscles recover faster after a workout.

Doping Is Never Accidental

Sometimes athletes who are caught doping attempt to explain their actions by saying they did not know the substance was an illegal steroid or was a banned substance. Barry Bonds told the grand jury investigating him for perjury that he never knew the substances he was taking were illegal steroids. Mark Fainaru-Wada and Lance Williams, who broke the story in the *San Francisco Chronicle* that the Bay Area Laboratory Co-Op (BALCO) was making and distributing undetectable steroids, dispute that claim. They write: "Bonds's approach was obvious: He didn't know what he put in his body, he simply ingested whatever substance his trainer gave him. If his trainer told him it was flaxseed oil and arthritis cream, then that's what it was. To people who knew Bonds's meticulous and controlling nature, the claim was absurd."

Mark Fainaru-Wada and Lance Williams, *Game of Shadows: Barry Bonds, BALCO, and the Steroids Scandal That Rocked Professional Sports*. New York: Gotham, 2006, p. 222.

San Francisco Chronicle *reporters Mark Fainaru-Wada, left, and Lance Williams wrote the book* Game of Shadows *about the BALCO steroid scandal.*

According to Alva Noe, a philosophy professor at the University of California–Berkeley:

> Discipline, determination, drive, a willingness to put in the hard hours of training and studying the game—those are the fruits of human labor, and we credit players for rising to the challenge. I think part of what offends the sports fan is the idea that steroids and human growth hormone are a substitute for hard work. . . . You'd have to be crazy to think steroids or other performance-enhancing drugs are a substitute for hard work. As with any worthwhile bit of human technology, steroids are effective only if used correctly; they work only in a context; indeed, they work only in the context of the training regimen of the athlete.[48]

What Caminiti, Bonds, Noe, and others contend is that the athlete must have the natural ability to be a great athlete. Taking steroids will not transform someone who has never played a sport before into a superstar.

"Natural" Enhancements

Those who believe that steroids are just another training aid contend that taking a performance-enhancing substance is no different from any other way of improving natural ability. These athletes argue that if athletes are allowed to use surgery or high-altitude training to enhance their skills, then athletes should also be permitted to use pharmaceutical aids such as steroids. Surgery, high-altitude training, and steroids all give athletes a competitive edge over athletes who have not taken advantage of these benefits. Tiger Woods underwent LASIK eye surgery to improve his vision to 20/15, which means he can see at a distance of 20 feet (6m) what most people can see at 15 feet (4.6m). The surgery was not much of a change for Woods, who was already wearing contact lenses that gave him 20/15 vision. Being able to see the lay of the land more clearly in golf, or the trajectory of a pitch in baseball, would give the athlete an immense advantage over other players whose vision is not as good. One sportswriter asked rhetorically, "If laser surgery, why not steroids?"[49]

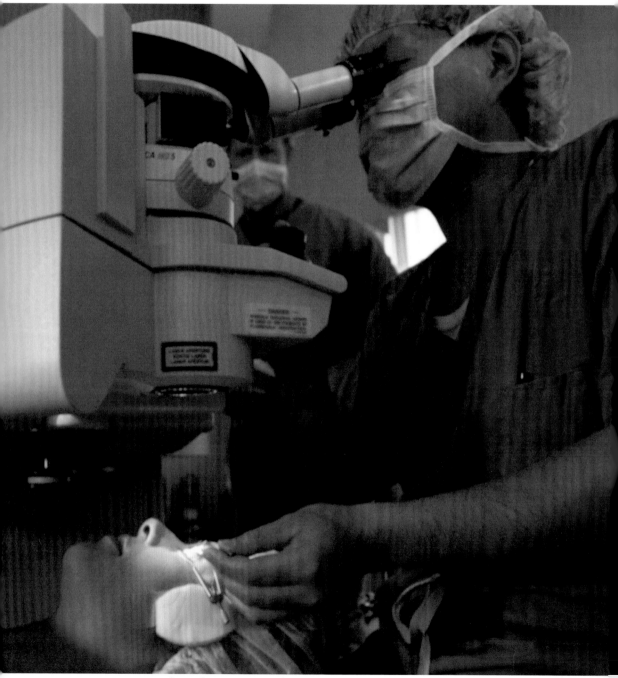

Proponents of steroids as a training aid contend that using the drug is no different from using other technologies, such as LASIK, that enhance performance.

Another surgical enhancement was the elbow surgery that pitcher Tommy John (and dozens of other baseball players after him) underwent to repair the tendon in his elbow, and which, incidentally, allowed him to throw the baseball harder than he did before the surgery. A sportswriter concluded, "We admire athletes who work hard, even risking injury, to improve their play. It is oddly paradoxical to damn those who do just that—albeit pharmaceutically."[50] Another common, and perhaps the most acceptable, enhancement is drinking coffee, tea, or cola for the caffeine in order to feel more alert.

STEROIDS ARE HERE TO STAY

"I have no doubt whatsoever that intelligent, informed use of steroids, combined with human growth hormone, will one day be so accepted that everybody will be doing it. Steroid use will be more common than Botox is now. Every baseball player and pro athlete will be using at least low levels of steroids."—Jose Canseco, former Major League Baseball player and admitted steroids user.

Jose Canseco, *Juiced: Wild Times, Rampant 'Roids, Smash Hits, and How Baseball Got Big.* New York: HarperCollins, 2005, p. 2.

Some question the difference between high-altitude training and the hormone erythropoietin, both of which stimulate the production of red blood cells and help improve an athlete's endurance and stamina. Many endurance athletes train at high altitudes, where oxygen levels in the air are extremely low. High-altitude training stimulates the production of oxygen-carrying red blood cells; when the athletes come back down to lower elevations, their blood still has higher levels of red blood cells, which improves their endurance. Jacob Sullum, author of *Saying Yes: In Defense of Drug Use*, is not sure that these methods of enhancing ability are any more ethical or have any more integrity than using steroids. "Everybody ought to be able to use the same tools. But I don't see what is different in principle between steroids and anything else artificial we do to change our abilities, be it working out, diet, the various medicines people take to recover from injuries."[51]

A "Sport Arms Race"

When athletes take performance-enhancing drugs and get that edge that will make them just a fraction of a second faster or a little bit stronger, other athletes may feel they also have to take steroids just to remain competitive. Thomas H. Murray, president of the Hastings Center, a bioethics research institute, compares athletes taking performance-enhancing drugs to an arms race. "The dynamics of drugs in sport bear more than a superficial resemblance to an arms race: each party drives the other further, lest either be left behind." While some argue that if all athletes were allowed to take steroids and other performance-enhancing substances it would level the playing field, Murray and others contend that such a change would come with a high cost to the athletes. "Athletes, caught in the sport arms race, would be pressed to take more and more drugs, in ever wilder combinations and at increasingly higher doses,"[52] which could be risky to athletes' health, Murray maintains. Moreover, many athletes want to play clean and not be drugged up with different performance enhancers. These clean athletes are in a no-win situation. If they play clean, they are at a competitive disadvantage. If they take steroids and other performance-enhancing substances, they risk their health, their career (most sports ban athletes who are caught using steroids), and their reputations. In addition, because some high-profile athletes use steroids, many people assume that all elite athletes take performance-enhancing substances, thus tarnishing the reputations of those who do not.

Rules in Sports

Almost all sports organizations, both amateur and professional, ban the use of steroids and other performance-enhancing substances. Athletes who take them are therefore violating the rules of their sport. Richard Pound, the founder of the World Anti-Doping Agency, which tests Olympic athletes for banned substances, says that the rules regulating sports is one of the most important elements of the game. The rules may be arbitrary and artificial, he says (such as the size and weight of equipment), but they are rules that the participants agree to abide by. Those who do not respect the rules, who try to get an unfair advantage over their competitors, are cheaters, he asserts. Pound writes in his book *Inside Dope: How Drugs Are the Biggest Threat to Sports, Why You Should Care, and What Can Be Done About Them*: "Cheaters are the sociopaths of sport. . . . All that matters to them is winning at any cost, and they are willing to cheat or willing to be persuaded to cheat in order to win."[53] According to Pound, they do not care about the promises they made to play clean, and their decision to use steroids and other performance-enhancing substances shows that they do not respect their fellow athletes, either.

STEROIDS MAKE A CONVENIENT SCAPEGOAT

"Baseball over the past decade and a half has seen no end of changes that may account for the rise in home runs often attributed to steroids. Expansion and newer (though not necessarily smaller) ballparks may be contributing factors, though neither completely explains the rise."—Will Carroll, author of *The Juice: The Real Story of Baseball's Drug Problem*, on other factors that may explain the increase in home runs in baseball.

Will Carroll, *The Juice: The Real Story of Baseball's Drug Problem*. Chicago: Ivan R. Dee, 2005, p. 229.

Many people contend, however, that the argument against a ban on steroids in sports is a circular argument. They assert that according to the circular argument, steroids are illegal because they are bad, and steroids are bad because they are illegal. The reason for the conclusion is simply a restatement of the conclusion. These statements are accepted as fact even though no evidence supports them, just unsubstantiated assertions from someone who claims a particular statement (steroids are bad) as fact. Along these lines are the arguments that using steroids is immoral and wrong. Joe Lindsey, a contributing writer for *Bicycling* magazine, has written widely

Richard Pound, founder of the World Anti-Doping Agency, argues that athletes who violate the agreed-upon rules of the sport are cheaters.

about performance-enhancing substances in professional cycling. He writes in an online article, "Doping in sports isn't inherently wrong; it's wrong by the value system with which we judge sports."[54]

Pound responds to this argument by asserting, once again, that "sport cannot exist without rules. And that's the whole point. They *are* the agreed-upon rules."[55] The rules against doping were developed after many years of studying the issue, he says, and after officials determined that drugs and performance enhancements harm the athletes in physical, psychological, and social ways. Lindsey echoes the conclusions of many when he asks, "Do you want to see who's the best athlete, or just who had the best access to pharmaceutical enhancement?"[56]

CHAPTER 4

REGULATING STEROID USE

M ost athletic and sporting organizations contend that steroids give athletes an unfair advantage over athletes who have not used the performance-enhancing drugs. To ensure that the winning athletes have won because of their natural skills, and not because of pharmaceutically enhanced skills, most sporting organizations have banned the use of steroids and other performance-enhancing drugs in their sports. However, the sporting organizations soon discovered that it was difficult to enforce the prohibition against illegal drug use.

Steroids Are Banned in Sports

The problem with banning drugs is that the organization must have some way of backing up the ban. Simply because an organization such as the International Olympic Committee (IOC) or Major League Baseball (MLB) says that athletes may not take steroids does not mean the athletes will stop taking performance enhancers. One of the first organizations to ban doping in sporting competitions was the International Association of Athletics Federations, which banned performance enhancements in 1928. However, no method for testing for banned substances had yet been developed, so athletes competed on the honor system. Eventually, by the mid-1960s a few tests had been developed for detecting drug use. When ways actually to test athletes for violations of the doping ban existed, more organizations began to prohibit athletes from taking performance-enhancing substances. The governing organizations for soccer and bicycling banned doping in 1966. The IOC followed suit the next year and placed

Canada's Ben Johnson set a 100-meter dash world record and won Olympic gold in 1988. He was stripped of his records and medals due to his steroid use.

steroids on its list of banned substances in 1975. Testing for steroids became much more prevalent in later years after some Communist bloc countries, such as East Germany, began implementing a secret state-sponsored doping program in order to win medals at the Olympics. Sensing that the athletes' sudden and amazing results were due to performance-enhancing drugs, IOC officials were determined to develop drug tests that could prove the athletes were taking steroids and therefore cheating.

Ben Johnson Stripped of His Gold Medal

One of the most notorious early doping scandals in the sports world centered on Canadian sprinter Ben Johnson at the Summer Olympic Games in Seoul, South Korea, in 1988. In the early 1980s Johnson had lost many important 100-meter races to American sprinter Carl Lewis. In 1985 Johnson started winning his races against Lewis and setting world records by just hundredths of a second. Johnson beat Lewis at the World Championships in Rome in 1987 by one-tenth of a second, setting a new world record. After this loss, Lewis said, without naming names, that he, too, could win if he was taking drugs. The rivalry between the two sprinters made their matchup at the Olympics a highly anticipated event. Johnson ran the 100-meter race in another world-record time of 9.79 seconds for the gold medal; Lewis, with a time of 9.92 seconds—an American record—had to settle for second place. But three days later it was revealed that Johnson had tested positive for steroids, and he was stripped of his gold medal, which was then given to Lewis. Johnson later admitted he had been using steroids at the time of the 1987 World Championship race, and he was stripped of that win as well.

After this scandal, Congress passed the Anti-Drug Abuse Act of 1988 that changed the penalty for possessing or distributing steroids without a prescription from a misdemeanor to a felony. All fifty states had already passed laws controlling all aspects of anabolic steroid use, including manufacturing, distributing, possessing, and prescribing. Then in 1990 Congress passed the Anabolic Steroid Control Act that made steroids a Schedule III drug. (Schedule III drugs are drugs that have a medical purpose and have a low to moderate potential for abuse or addiction.) The categorization of steroids as a Schedule III drug made it a federal crime to use, possess, sell, or dispense steroids without a prescription.

Opposition to Steroid Regulation

The conversion of steroids from a prescription medicine to a controlled substance with all kinds of regulations governing its distribution and possession did not go unopposed. The directors of the Drug Enforcement Agency and Health and Human Services

A Comparison of Penalties for Violations of Performance-Enhancing Drug Use

Professional sporting organizations in the United States have set their own rules and policies concerning steroid use. Not only do their policies differ on which drugs are and are not permitted, but the penalties each organization imposes for violations vary widely. Below is a sampling from a few major sports organizations:

Organization	1st violation	2nd violation	3rd violation	4th violation	5th violation
NFL (16 games in a regular season)	4 games min.	6 games	1 year	1 year	1 year
NBA (1999–2005) (82 games in a regular season)	5 games	10 games	25 games	25 games	25 games
NHL (2005) (82 games in a regular season)	20 games	60 games	Lifetime ban		
MLB (2005) (162 games in a regular season)	50 games	100 games	Lifetime ban		
Olympics	2 years	Lifetime ban			

Source: Mark Conrad, *The Business of Sports: A Primer for Journalists.* New York: Routledge, 2008, p. 242.

testified before a Senate Judiciary Committee that anabolic steroids did not meet the requirements to be classified as a Schedule III drug. In addition, the American Medical Association opposed making steroids a Schedule III drug because, according to the association's representative Edward Langston, "abuse of steroids does not lead to the physical or psychological dependence as is required for scheduling."[57] Nevertheless, Congress was persuaded by two arguments to reclassify steroids: Steroids give the athletes who use them an unfair advantage, and athletes who use steroids are sending a message to the nation's youth that it is acceptable to cheat to win.

A BAD JOKE?

"Well then, it's not cheating, is it? If nobody finds out?"—Danica Patrick, race car driver, joking about whether she would take performance-enhancing drugs if she would not get caught and if it would lead to her winning the Indianapolis 500 race.

Quoted in, Christine Brennan, "Danica Should Know That Cheating Is No Joke," *USA Today*, June 1, 2009, p. C3.

Other Doping Scandals

Despite the example set by stripping Ben Johnson of his gold medal, athletes continued to take steroids. One sport that is particularly plagued by doping scandals is professional cycling, especially the grueling Tour de France race, which has had allegations of doping nearly every year for over a decade. Entire teams have been eliminated due to drug raids and positive drug tests. In 1998 an assistant with a cycling team sponsored by the Festina watch manufacturer was arrested for possession of growth hormone, testosterone, amphetamines, and erythropoietin (a blood doping agent). Police raided hotels used by Tour de France cyclists and found more steroids and performance-enhancing substances. After arrests and withdrawals from the race, fewer than half the cyclists who started the race crossed the finish line.

The immense publicity and embarrassment following the Tour de France drug raids encouraged the IOC and various sporting organizations to coordinate their anti-doping efforts. Richard Pound, a former vice president of the IOC, founded the World Anti-Doping Agency (WADA). WADA is an independent and international drug testing agency supported by the IOC and participating nations. It researches new performance-enhancing substances and methods to detect them, provides education about doping in sports, and develops and monitors a list of substances that have been banned from sports.

Prior to the establishment of WADA, each sporting organization had its own list of banned substances and different penalties for using them. WADA has encouraged most international sporting federations and governing bodies to follow its Anti-Doping Code, which imposes extremely severe penalties on athletes who are caught doping. Athletes who are caught using steroids or other performance-enhancing substances are banned from participating in their sport for two years. A second offense is a lifetime ban.

Under the WADA Anti-Doping Code, athletes are 100 percent responsible for any banned substance found during drug tests:

> It is each Athlete's personal duty to ensure that no Prohibited Substance enters his or her body. Athletes are responsible for any Prohibited Substance . . . found to be present in their bodily specimens. Accordingly, it is not necessary that intent, fault, negligence, or knowing Use on the Athlete's part be demonstrated in order to establish an anti-doping violation.[58]

In other words, athletes will still be guilty of a doping violation if they take a "vitamin" pill from their coach or trainer, and the "vitamin" is actually a banned substance, or if they take a substance they did not know was prohibited under the WADA Anti-Doping Code. If banned substances are found during drug tests, the athlete is guilty, no matter how it came to be in the athlete's body.

The 1998 Tour de France was marred by participants' doping scandals.

Professional Sports Begin Drug Testing

Penalties for banned drug use are not nearly as severe in the professional sports leagues in the United States. In fact, actually getting professional athletes to submit to testing is not as easy as it is for the elite athletes such as Olympians, professional bicyclists, and track and field athletes. Professional athletes have used their collective bargaining agreements and players' unions to fight mandatory testing. Gradually, though, the professional sports organizations are beginning to require athletes to undergo drug testing, although some sports require testing only once a year. In addition, some require that only a small percentage of athletes, and not all of them, undergo testing.

The National Basketball Association was one of the first professional sporting organizations to initiate drug testing, in 1983. But more than twenty years later, the policy has remained essentially unchanged. Athletes are tested for illegal drugs and performance-enhancing substances only if evidence is uncovered that

Management Ignores the Evidence

Dan Clark performed on the television show *American Gladiator* for six seasons. During his stint as the gladiator Nitro, he and the other gladiators regularly used steroids to bulk up their muscles. After a scandal in the World Wrestling Federation, in which it was alleged that the chief executive officer was providing steroids to the wrestlers on his show, the gladiators were told they must take a drug test. Any gladiator who tested positive for steroids would be fired. The gladiators were then told the test would be in six weeks. Clark said:

I come to the stark realization that, just as in baseball and other professional sports, some of the producers of the Gladiators are not only willing to look the other way

when it comes to steroid use, they are willing to do what is necessary to protect their property. Unlike cocaine, which devalues the producer's property, steroids actually help—at least in the short term. When home runs are sailing over fences and bodies are flying around in the gladiator arena, the ratings go up and the revenue comes in. The producers have a good reason to look the other way. By giving us the test dates in advance, they are doing more than ignoring the evidence. They're implicitly giving us a chance to come off the drugs and pass the test.

Dan Clark, *Gladiator: A True Story of 'Roids, Rage, and Redemption.* New York: Scribner, 2009, p. 149.

demonstrates the athlete is using drugs. A basketball player who tests positive for steroids or marijuana must enter a substance-abuse program and is suspended for five games for a first offense (out of a possible eighty-two games in a regular season), ten games for a second offense, and twenty-five games for subsequent violations.

STATE PROGRAM TO TEST HIGH SCHOOL STUDENTS FOR STEROIDS IS A WINNER

"Whether there's no positives or a lot, [New Jersey's steroid testing program is] a winner. The more attention you draw to it and make students realize what's going to happen to them if they do steroids, the better off we are as a society."—Jackie Friedman, a sportswriter, on New Jersey's steroid testing program for high school students.

Jackie Friedman, "State's Steroid Testing: Is the Program Paying Off with the Right Result?" *Newark* (NJ) *Star-Ledger,* May 24, 2009. http://highschoolsports.nj.com/news/article/5102384832741845801/steroid-testing-in-hs-sports/.

The National Football League began testing its players in 1990. A computer randomly selects six players from each team to be tested each week. Players who test positive for steroids or performance-enhancing substances receive a four-game suspension; a six-game suspension is given for a second violation, and a third positive drug test results in a one-year suspension. In addition, if a drug test result shows the presence of a "masking" agent (a drug typically taken to cover up the presence of an illegal drug or steroid), even if no steroid is detected, the player receives the appropriate suspension as well. Suspensions in football are a little more serious than basketball, as there are sixteen games in a regular season.

Major League Baseball

Major League Baseball was one of the last sporting organizations to crack down on its players who use performance-enhancing drugs. Prior to 1986 players were not subjected to any kind of

In 1983 the National Basketball Association was one of the first sports organizations to institute a drug testing policy.

drug testing. Since 1986 testing players for drug use was included in collective bargaining agreements with the Major League Players Association, which opposed mandatory random drug testing of ballplayers due to privacy concerns. A sports reporter wrote about seeing the steroid androstenedione in Mark McGwire's locker in 1998, but steroids were not banned at the time, and Major League Baseball did not punish him for it. Finally in 2002, baseball players agreed to submit to a drug testing survey that determined that 5 to 7 percent of baseball players used steroids and other performance-enhancing substances (although some insiders say the percentage of steroid users is much higher). The drug test results were supposed to be anonymous, and no player would be disciplined for steroid use. That confidentiality was breached in 2009, though, when *Sports Illustrated* magazine revealed that Alex Rodriguez had tested positive for steroids in the anonymous survey.

MANY WAYS TO CHEAT ON A STEROID TEST

"There are many ways to beat the tests. For many years, cheaters smuggled in clean urine, hidden on their person or in bladders concealed in body cavities, which they provided instead of their own. That is one of the reasons why doping control officers are required to observe that the sample is provided properly."—Richard Pound, the founder of the World Anti-Doping Agency, on some of the ways athletes try to avoid detection of their steroid use during tests.

Richard Pound, *Inside Dope: How Drugs Are the Biggest Threat to Sports, Why You Should Care, and What Can Be Done About Them.* Mississauga, ON: Wiley, 2006, p. 85.

Until 2004 baseball players who tested positive did not face any kind of penalty for using a banned substance. In 2004 players who did test positive for steroids and other banned drugs were sent to a counselor. The following year the policy was changed again to a ten-game suspension, and twelve players—including Rafael Palmeiro, who nearly five months earlier had testified before Congress, "I have never used steroids. Period."[59]

On March 17, 2005, Rafael Palmeiro of the Baltimore Orioles testified before the U.S. Congress that he had never used steroids. Five months later he tested positive.

—were suspended for testing positive for steroids. After the 2005 season had ended, the suspensions were changed again, this time to fifty games, and since then, seventeen more players have been suspended, including Manny Ramirez, who was suspended in May 2009. Ramirez is just the most recent—and perhaps the highest profile—professional baseball player to be suspended for using a banned substance. Baseball has gone from having one of the lightest suspension policies to one of the strictest, since there are 162 games in a regular season. A player who is suspended for fifty games is out for nearly a third of the season.

Policy Questions

The suspension of Ramirez reignited the debate about Major League Baseball's antidrug policy. While the 2002 confidential survey commissioned by MLB found that 5 to 7 percent of professional ballplayers used steroids, former player and admitted steroid user Jose Canseco asserts that when he was playing in the late 1990s, the number was closer to 80 percent. The huge discrepancy between the two numbers leads to the question of whether baseball's antidrug policy is finally harsh enough to stop players from doping, or if it is still too lax and lenient and therefore players have little to fear about getting caught. Gary I. Wadler, a New York sports medicine expert and key official with WADA, contends that while Major League Baseball's antidrug policy has made great progress in the past decade, "it's still not where it needs to be." WADA officials have consistently criticized MLB's antidrug policy as "a complete and utter joke." Until 2007 the maximum penalty for steroid use was a one-year suspension; that was changed to a lifetime suspension after a third violation. Wadler contends that Major League Baseball will not give players who test positive for steroids a two-year suspension because the owners are too worried about profit and loss: "The pro leagues can't see their superstars being sanctioned for two years. But if you're really serious about getting doping out of your sport, you've got to bite the bullet."[60]

Defenders of baseball's new steroid policy disagree with Wadler's assertions. They contend that Major League Baseball is finally serious about ending steroid abuse among its players. According to one MLB official, giving a fifty-game suspension to Manny Ramirez, a potential Hall of Famer and twelve-time All-Star player with more than five hundred home runs, proves that the rules are being enforced and that star players are not receiving special treatment. It was the most severe punishment Major

In his testimony before Congress, Dr. Gary Wadler of WADA stated that while Major League Baseball has made progress with its antidrug policy "it is still not where it needs to be."

League Baseball had ever given one of its players. In addition, Ramirez was forced to give up his salary while he was suspended, which means he lost about $7.7 million, or nearly one-third of his $25 million salary.

Drug Testing in High School and College

Professional and elite-level athletes are not the only athletes who are tested for performance-enhancing drugs. Testing for steroids has spread to colleges and high schools as well. While some of the

Baseball Commissioner
Testifies Before Congress

The commissioner of Major League Baseball, Bud Selig, authorized a report known as the Mitchell Report to study steroid use in baseball. In January 2008 Selig testified before Congress about how the attitudes in baseball have changed from the "anything goes" era of Jose Canseco, who claimed that approximately 80 percent of ballplayers were using steroids in the late 1990s:

> Baseball now has the strongest drug testing program in professional sports. Our penalty structure of 50 games, 100 games and life is the toughest. We test for stimulants, including amphetamines. We have year-round, unannounced testing, including testing on game days, both before and after games. We use the Olympic-certified laboratories in Montreal for our testing and the day-to-day administration of the program has been delegated to an Independent Program Administrator. A whole generation of players has grown up under our strict Minor League testing policy, which is entering its eighth season. As a result of all of this, our positive tests have declined significantly from 96 in the 2003 survey test to just two steroid positives in 2006 and three in 2007. This improvement is similar to what we have observed in our Minor League program under which the positive rate declined from nine percent in 2001 to less than one-half of one percent in 2007. Just last week, I met with a group of 12 certified athletic trainers from Major League Clubs who assured me that we have changed the culture in Clubhouses regarding steroid use.

Statement of Commissioner Allan H. "Bud" Selig before the House Committee on Oversight and Government Reform, January 15, 2008. http://oversight.house.gov/documents/20080115114736.pdf.

In January 2008 Major League Baseball commissioner Bud Selig testified before Congress that MLB now has the strongest drug testing program in professional sports.

issues of drug testing are the same at this level, there are additional concerns about testing younger athletes. The percentage of athletes who use steroids at the college and high school level is reputed to be fairly low. According to the 2007 Monitoring the Future survey, the prevalence of steroid use among students in eighth grade to age twenty-eight varies from 1.5 percent of eighth graders to a high of 2.2 percent of twelfth graders. Only 1.7 percent of young adults aged nineteen to twenty-eight admitted in the confidential and anonymous survey that they used steroids. Add to that the high costs of testing, which range from $50 to $150 per test, and many people argue that testing for steroids is a waste of money that could be better used on other things.

QUESTIONS ON WHETHER IT IS POSSIBLE TO RUN A CLEAN RACE

"Some people think the Tour is so brutal that no one can win it without chemical help. In some quarters, the continued doping scandals of this year's race suggest that the entire enterprise may be doomed to corruption."—Jack Ewing, Frankfurt bureau chief for *BusinessWeek* magazine, on using performance-enhancing drugs in the Tour de France bicycle race.

Jack Ewing, "Tour de France Raises Fresh Questions About Honesty in Sports," *BusinessWeek*, July 25, 2008. www.businessweek.com/globalbiz/blog/europeinsight/archives/2008/07/tour_de_france.html.

Texas, Florida, Illinois, and New Jersey require high school athletes be tested for steroids. Texas began its testing program in February 2008, and by the end of the fall 2008 semester had tested nearly twenty-nine thousand student athletes. Only eleven high school athletes tested positive for steroids. Florida suspended its steroid testing program after one year because there was only one positive result out of six hundred students tested. An Associated Press survey of steroid tests in the four states found that only 18 tests out of 30,799 came back positive. School administrators and state legislators in the four states called the testing program a great success, claiming the tests work as a deterrent to steroid use. State representative Dan Flynn, who sponsored the Texas legislation that authorized the testing, said, "This means that the program is working because the kids know they are being tested and stayed away from steroids."[61]

Critics of testing high school athletes assert, however, that the tests are a waste of money. Matt Bartle, a state senator from

State-by State Look at High School Steroid Test Results

Four states have begun mandatory testing of high school students for steroids. The criteria for which students will be tested varies from state to state. Texas plans to test all student athletes; New Jersey tests only a few athletes from the teams that make it to the state championship level. Florida discontinued its testing after only one year because the number of positive test results was so low: one.

Florida
Tests administered: 600
Positive results: 1
Note: Florida had a statewide testing program only during the 2007–2008 school year.

Illinois
Tests administered: 264
Positive results: 6
Note: The program began in the fall of 2008; results reflect only

one semester of testing. All six students who tested positive had medical exemptions.

New Jersey
Tests administered: 1,001
Positive results: 2
Note: Results reflect 2006–2007 and 2007–2008 school years.

Texas
Tests administered: 28,934
Positive results: 11
Note: Results reflect spring 2008 and fall 2008 semesters. Additionally, there were 12 unresolved tests sent for review and 70 "process positives" in which students had unexcused absences, refused to give samples, or left testing sites.

Source: Geoff Mulvihill, "Few Caught by Steroid Testing in High School," March 17, 2009. www.standard.net.

Missouri, tried to convince his colleagues to pass a steroid testing program for high school athletes, but when he saw Florida's results, he abandoned the proposal. "Is there enough steroid use out there that spending a couple million bucks a year against everything else that the state needs to spend money on is worth it?"[62] he asked. Texas spent $6 million to test fifty thousand students over two years. Critics say the low number of positive results do not justify the expense.

Moreover, in a study of 197 college student athletes who all volunteered to undergo testing for steroid use, and who all claimed to be clean, 2 athletes tested positive for steroids. The study's authors, Russell Meldrum and Judy Feinberg, assert that this result shows that testing is not a deterrent to drug use. Despite receiving education on the dangers of steroid use, Meldrum and Feinberg argue, "the decision to not use drugs is felt to be related more to the fear of reprisal than to health issues." Moreover, they assert, "the use of anabolic steroids among athletes, although not increasing, has not diminished under the current testing programs."[63]

Peer Pressure

Experts on steroid use agree that the best way to prevent or deter steroid use is through peer pressure. Testing is not "a quick fix," said Linn Goldberg, a doctor who specializes in sports medicine. "There has to be peer pressure to do the right thing."[64] Teens who go through drug education programs together often exert peer pressure on each other to stay clean. Two proven programs are ATLAS and ATHENA, offered by the Oregon Health and Science University. ATLAS is geared toward male athletes, while ATHENA is for females. The university trains the coaches in the principles of the program, but the student athletes are the program's true leaders. The program offers the athletes information on sports nutrition and strength-training exercises. In addition, the student leaders work with their fellow students on role-playing ways to refuse steroids and other drugs, creating campaigns or public service announcements, playing interactive games, and setting goals. The National Institute on Drug Abuse, a government organization that studies drug abuse and addiction, studied more than 3,200 students who had gone through ATLAS and ATHENA a year earlier and found that steroid use among those who had gone through the programs had declined by more than 50 percent. The students said they learned how to stand up for themselves and say no to using steroids. According to Goldberg, the approach used by these programs "exerts positive peer pressure and promotes positive role modeling."[65]

CHAPTER 5

WHAT IS THE FUTURE OF STEROIDS IN SPORTS?

One of the greatest scandals involving steroids in sports illustrates how difficult it is to keep up with the development of new performance-enhancing drugs. In the summer of 2002, a routine urine sample sent for testing to a drug analysis laboratory near Los Angeles made the chemists sit up and take notice. The lab was the Olympic Analytical Laboratory at the University of California–Los Angeles, which had been established prior to the 1984 Olympic Games in Los Angeles to test the athletes for prohibited performance-enhancing drugs. On first glance this particular urine sample seemed to show no signs of any steroids or banned substances. But scientists thought something in the sample looked off, and so they ran another test on it. The second test showed the presence of a steroid known as norethandrolone. The scientists were surprised at the presence of this drug, since norethandrolone, which had originally been patented by Wyeth Pharmaceuticals during the 1960s, had never been commercially manufactured. It had been abandoned and forgotten about for thirty-five years before showing up in the drug test of American cyclist Tammy Thomas.

According to Don H. Catlin, director of the Olympic Analytical Laboratory, there were two possible scenarios for the reemergence of this steroid. "One," he said, "there was a scientist from Wyeth who had squirreled away a supply" and had kept quiet on its existence for decades, a possibility he felt did not make much sense. "Or," he mused, "there was a rogue scientist out there making it."[66] Catlin experimented and discovered that the steroid could be easily made by someone who had the right equipment and ingredients. It was then that Catlin realized that science would be continually trying to detect new and previously undetectable versions of banned performance-enhancing substances. The steroid business had suddenly become very sophisticated.

The BALCO Scandal

The next summer Trevor Graham, a well-known track coach, called the U.S. Anti-Doping Agency (USADA), the organization that coordinates and manages all the drug testing for the U.S.

Dr. Donald Catlin is the director of the Olympic Analytical Library at UCLA. He admits that science has a lot of catching up to do in order to detect newly banned substances.

Olympic Games, to say he knew several high-profile track stars who were using undetectable performance-enhancing drugs. He sent a syringe with some residue in the needle to the USADA office, which in turn sent it to Catlin's laboratory in Los Angeles for identification. Catlin assured Rich Wanninger at USADA that the substance was probably harmless; his lab received unknown materials all the time that usually turned out to be nothing. Wanninger, however, was convinced that it was a new drug, and with the U.S. Track and Field Championships just a few days away, he wanted an immediate answer as to whether it was a performance-enhancing drug so that the athletes could be tested for it.

Catlin soon discovered that the substance was indeed a new and previously undetectable steroid. The steroid was closely related to two other known steroids, but its molecular structure had been deliberately altered to avoid detection during standard drug tests. Catlin named the designer steroid tetrahydrogestrinone, or THG, and created a test to detect it. The new drug test was created just in time for the track and field championships. Catlin's lab secretly tested samples from athletes who competed at the championships and found four positive results. All of the positive results came from athletes who were national champions in their sport: shot-putter Kevin Toth, hammer throwers John McEwen and Melissa Price, and middle-distance runner Regina Jacobs.

The USADA did not announce the results of the tests yet; it was hoping to test more athletes to discover who was using the steroid before word leaked out about its discovery. The International Association of Athletics Federations immediately collected samples from several prominent international athletes, including Dwain Chambers, a British sprinter, and Kelli White, an American sprinter. These athletes and others who were subsequently discovered to be using THG—baseball players Barry Bonds, Jason Giambi, and Gary Sheffield; Oakland Raiders football players Bill Romanowski, Tyrone Wheatley, and Chris Cooper; and cyclist Tammy Thomas—all bought supplements from the same source: the Bay Area Laboratory Co-Operative (BALCO), a nutritional supplements company based in the San Francisco Bay area, owned by Victor Conte.

BALCO owner Victor Conte marketed and sold THG as the "Clear" that could not be detected by drug tests.

The Clear and the Cream

Conte bought THG from a chemist on the East Coast, Patrick Arnold, who created the new steroid in order to avoid detection during routine drug tests. Conte marketed and sold THG as the "Clear" to his athlete clients. The Clear was not actually clear, but a mixture of flaxseed oil and steroids that was caramel in color. Athletes took the Clear by placing a few drops of the steroid under the tongue. It was called the Clear because athletes who used it were cleared during their drug tests.

CLEAN ATHLETES ARE TAINTED BY ATHLETES WHO DOPE

"Any time somebody tests positive in track and field, it's a major blow. It doesn't matter if it's during the Olympic trials or the Olympics, or Christmas, or whenever. It's a huge blow. . . . Quite frankly, it sucks. It really does."—Terrence Trammel, an American hurdler who won the silver medal at the 2000 and 2004 Olympics, on the effect steroid-using athletes have on clean athletes.

Quoted in Alan Abrahamson, "Project Believe," *NBC Sports Blogs*, April 16, 2008. http://blogs.nbcsports.com/home/archives/2008/04/project-believe.html.

Conte sold another steroid he called the "Cream." The Cream contained testosterone and epitestosterone ("epi") in a lotion that was rubbed on the athlete's skin. The Cream was used to mask the presence of steroids taken by the athlete. Steroids suppress the body's natural production of testosterone. One way to detect the presence of steroids in an athlete's body is to test for the presence of testosterone and epitetosterone. Epi is another naturally occurring substance in the body, although scientists do not know its exact function. Epi and testosterone occur in a one-to-one ratio. However, in athletes who take steroids, the epi-to-testosterone ratio changes. When the ratio is higher than six to one, or even four to one in some sports, the athlete is considered to be doping. The Cream works to even out the epi-testosterone ratio, thus masking the presence of steroids in the body.

Differences in Penalties

The Cream and the Clear symbolize the difficulties inherent in catching steroid users. Rogue chemists are continually tinkering with the formulations for steroids, trying to create new drugs and performance-enhancing substances that will evade detection in

"I Have Never Tested Positive for Steroids"

Marion Jones, who won three gold and two bronze medals in track at the 2000 Olympics in Sydney, was implicated in the BALCO steroid scandal by Victor Conte, the owner of the Bay Area Laboratory Co-Op. Through an anonymous tip, Conte was discovered to be selling an undetectable steroid to his clients, who included Marion Jones, Barry Bonds, and Bill Romanowski, among others. Jones denied the allegations of steroid use to the press and to a grand jury investigating the BALCO scandal, saying:

My response all along is the fact I've never accepted nor taken nor been offered any performance-enhancing drug from anyone. . . . That's the truth. That's what I'm going to stick with. . . . My life does not revolve around having to prove to anyone that I am drug free. I am probably one of the most tested athletes in the world. I have never tested positive for a steroid. The people that know me . . . know I would never do anything illegal. I would never take any performance-enhancing drug. I'm not going to degrade myself to prove I'm drug free. I know I am.

Jones was convicted in 2007 of lying to the grand jury and was sentenced to six months in jail. She was also stripped of her wins and medal from the 2000 Olympics.

Quoted in John Crumpacker, "Marion Jones Isn't Running from Steroid Controversy," *San Francisco Chronicle*, May 14, 2004. www.sfgate.com/cgi-bin/article.cgi%3Ff%3D/chronicle/archive/2004/05/14/SPGN86L3NH1.DTL.

Olympic gold medalist Marion Jones was convicted of lying to federal prosecutors about her steroid use and was sentenced to six months in prison.

drug tests. While steroids are a controlled substance, the penalties for those who create and sell new, undetectable steroids are light. Arnold was sentenced to three months in prison and three months' home confinement for creating the Clear; Conte, who sold it, received a four-month prison sentence.

PROGRAM CLEANS UP SPORTS

"There's no way you can make a 1,000 percent guarantee that everyone is clean. But hearing from athletes, they feel a lot more strongly that they have an equal chance of winning now without having to dope, and that's very important."—Travis Tygart, chief executive officer of the U.S. Anti-Doping Agency, on the agency's new program that tests selected athletes to ensure they are not doping.

Quoted in Eddie Pells, "USADA Won't Rest Despite Presumably Clean Olympics," *USA Today*, September 25, 2008. www.usatoday.com/sports/olympics/2008-09251133210969_x.htm.

The penalties for athletes who use steroids in amateur or elite-level sports are much harsher, on the other hand. For athletes who compete in the Olympics and their sport's national championships, getting caught using steroids means an automatic two-year suspension. A second offense will ban them for life. Professional athletes, for the most part, do not face such strict penalties for steroid use, although most professional sports are increasing their penalties. Most professional sports suspend an athlete without pay for a specified number of games, with each subsequent violation earning a higher number of games suspended.

Many professional athletes believe it is worth the risk to take "undetectable" steroids. Those who use these new designer steroids get all the benefits of using steroids—increased muscle mass, increased strength, faster recovery from workouts—with little worry of getting caught by drug tests. Romanowski, the former Oakland Raiders football player who was caught using the Clear during the BALCO scandal, said he "took considerable pride in trying to outsmart the system. . . . I was taking performance-

Former NFL player Bill Romanowski, who was caught up in the BALCO scandal, says that he would stop taking a banned substance as soon as he found out tests could detect it.

enhancing substances they couldn't test for, like THG. As soon as I found out something could be tested for, I stopped taking it."[67]

SCHOOLS MUST CHANGE IDEAS OF WHAT IS CONSIDERED ACCEPTABLE

"It helps change the culture in the athletic departments about what is acceptable. . . . Changing the norm in their environment is one of the hardest things to do, and you can't just depend on outside information to do it."—Timothy Condin, associate director at the National Institute on Drug Abuse, on the ATLAS (Athletes Training & Learning to Avoid Steroids) program in high schools.

Quoted in Lya Wodraska, "Just Say Yes," *Teacher* magazine, April 1, 2002. www.teacher magazine.org/tm/articles/2002/04/01/07atlas.h13.html?tkn=ZQRDHVF9kRb36F0 AFvr7BZIUkWB8VfHbtysd.

A *Washington Post* study found that it is extremely easy to find new steroids that are currently undetectable in drug tests. The newspaper bought five nutritional supplements online that were advertised to build muscles fast. It then asked Catlin's drug testing lab at the University of California–Los Angeles to analyze the supplements; Catlin found that four of the five supplements were previously unknown steroids. Catlin's laboratory was aware of the fifth steroid, but researchers did not know it was available for purchase by the general public. One official with a nutritional supplement company said it was easy to fool drug testers. "There's an unlimited pool of steroids," he said. "You could do this for the next 100 years. . . . The longer they don't pay attention the [more rampant] it gets."[68] Moreover, officials with both drug testing labs and supplement companies agree that the light sentences imposed in the BALCO scandal embolden others to get into the field of selling steroids as nutritional supplements.

Furthermore, even the drug testers acknowledge that testing for steroids is a never-ending game of catch-up. Athlete Nathan Jendrick, author of *Dunks, Doubles, Doping*, writes, "As soon as the drug testers catch on to one drug, there will likely be another that is undetectable."[69] It is, he writes, a "cat and mouse game of cheaters trying to stay ahead of the drug testers" which is "a recipe for disaster."[70] By constantly altering and tweaking the composition of steroids to come up with new designer steroids, the creators do not know what effects these changes will have on the human body when they are ingested.

Alternatives to Drug Testing

Since it is not yet possible for drug testers to design a test to detect steroids that do not exist yet, or that are not known to exist, some people believe there must be other ways to end doping in sports. Catlin, who has been testing athletes for illegal substances since 1984, believes there must be a better way. "Science can't solve all the problems," he says. "For me—who . . . believed we

The "I Have Never Tested Positive" Myth Exploded

Many athletes who are accused of taking steroids often respond to the accusation by saying "I have never tested positive." Richard Pound, founder of the World Anti-Doping Agency, explains why people should not take this response as proof that the athlete is "clean" and has never doped:

> "I have never tested positive" has become so commonplace that it is a wonder anyone was ever fooled by it. This statement is trotted out as proof that the athletes in question have not doped—no positive result means no doping. End of any possible

controversy, they say. But, the statement is true only as far as its contents take it. The only thing it proves is exactly what it says— that the person has never tested positive. It doesn't prove whether or not the person has used the prohibited substances or methods. It simply means that they never got caught if they were doping. Often, it was because there was no test at the time for the substance they were using.

Richard Pound, *Inside Dope: How Drugs Are the Biggest Threat to Sports, Why You Should Care, and What Can Be Done About Them.* Mississauga, ON: Wiley, 2006, pp. 84–85.

could do it just with doping control and testing—to say it's not working is a bit of a change."[71] Catlin experimented with an idea that rewards athletes for staying clean instead of punishing them for doping.

His Volunteer Program would make athletes prove that they are clean, rather than having scientists prove they are doping. In his program, athletes would be tested frequently. Their test results would form a baseline biological profile. Any spike in the athlete's levels of testosterone, hemoglobin, or other body chemistry levels would indicate drug use, even if traditional drug tests showed no indication of any banned substances.

While Catlin's Volunteer Program never got off the ground, a similar program, Project Believe, run by the USADA, was in place in time for the 2008 Summer Olympics in Beijing. Twelve athletes participated in the program, including decathlete Bryan Clay and swimmers Michael Phelps and Dara Torres. Torres, a forty-one-year-old swimmer who had already won gold medals in four previous Olympics, faced enormous scrutiny over her decision to return to racing. Many were suspicious that her record-breaking qualifying times were due to her use of illegal substances.

Project Believe

To prove that she was clean, Torres went to the USADA headquarters and met with Travis Tygart, the agency's chief executive officer, and demanded that she be tested. Tygart said he was skeptical when Torres appeared in his office asserting she was clean. He remembered that Marion Jones, an American track star who also had insisted she was clean, had had no indications of banned substances show up in her drug test results, but then was forced to admit during the BALCO scandal that she had used undetectable steroids obtained from BALCO. "You're telling us all the same stuff Marion told us when we met with her and you're saying all the right things,"[72] Tygart told Torres. "Why should I believe you?"[73] Torres responded by saying USADA could test her at any time and could use hair, urine, blood, or DNA so she could prove she was not using banned substances. "I decided to become an open book, and asked to be tested in any way they want to show I'm clean," she said. "I understand if I just sat there and

When forty-one-year-old Dara Torres qualified for the 2008 U.S. Olympic swim team, she volunteered to be tested under the Project Believe guidelines to assure officials that she was steroid free.

said I passed my tests, that people wouldn't believe me. I've gone beyond the call of duty to prove I'm clean, but you are guilty until proven innocent in this day and age, so what else can I do?"[74]

Tygart then told Torres about USADA's new program, Project Believe. While participating in the program, Torres provided urine and blood samples every couple of weeks, which tested her biological markers looking for signs of performance-enhancing substances. Although the results showed no signs that Torres had been using any kind of banned substances, USADA cannot guarantee she is not doping. "The science is not at the stage where we can give a 100 percent guarantee to any athlete that they are clean," Tygart said. "But if they aren't clean, then they would have to be a fool, or a huge risk taker to do a program like this."[75]

Culture Change

Athletes take steroids because they believe steroids will push them a little bit farther than they could get on their own, and the performance-enhancing substances help them be the best possible athlete they can be. Testing athletes for steroid use is unlikely to make a difference, as athletes will simply search out the latest drugs that are said to be undetectable. What is needed, according to Shaun Assael, author of *Steroid Nation*, is a culture change in how Americans view athletes who are caught doping. In addition, athletes must change the way they think about steroids, a requirement that will not be easy.

When a reporter wrote about discovering androstenedione in Mark McGwire's locker in 1998, many baseball fans shrugged it off as irrelevant to the home run race between McGwire and Sammy Sosa. Even the respected *New York Times* did not think that his use of what was then a legal nutritional supplement and is now classified as a steroid occurred under "questionable circumstances."[76] The prevailing attitude of both the public and the media, according to John Hoberman of the University of Texas–Austin, "was that the use of "Andro" was (a) a private matter and (b) irrelevant to the integrity of the game." Hoberman argues that the media coverage of McGwire's use of a disputed performance-enhancing substance "was only the latest evidence of our society's basically tolerant attitude toward doping"[77] in sports. He concludes that the public is more interested in sporting success stories than in sporting contests that are free of drugs.

Former baseball player and admitted steroid user Jose Canseco agrees wholeheartedly with Hoberman's assessment of what the public wants in sports. In his tell-all book *Juiced: Wild Times, Rampant 'Roids, Smash Hits, and How Baseball Got Big*, Canseco contends that not only did the public enjoy the home runs hit by steroid-using ballplayers, baseball management did, too. "Is it all that secret when owners of the game put out the word that they want home runs and excitement, making sure that everyone from trainers to managers to clubhouse attendants understands that whatever it is the players are doing to become superhuman, they sure ought to keep it up?"[78]

A PERPETUAL GAME OF CATCH-UP

"The trouble is that by the time the [International Olympic Committee] labs find the substance, do the testing necessary to make sure they can reliably detect it, and put it on the banned list, the athletes have moved on to another substance that may provide the same ergogenic [physically enhancing] effect."—Jim Ferstle, a journalist who specializes in writing about drug use in sports, on how steroid testers must constantly try to catch up with the latest steroids used by athletes.

Quoted in Charles Yesalis, ed., *Anabolic Steroids in Sport and Exercise*, 2nd ed. Champaign, IL: Human Kinetics, 2000, p. 395.

What this all means, according to Sanjay Gupta, a medical correspondent for several media outlets, is that athletes will not change their behavior concerning steroids until society changes its views about athletes who dope. Gupta explains: "You as the athlete have in your mind how you want to be remembered. That's why you put yourself through such excruciating pain day in and day out to get there. And if that legacy is on the line, if the political winds turn, and suddenly anybody associated with these things are looked at as bad people, in an era of cheating, that's the deterrent."[79]

Only when society's prevailing attitude is that athletes who use steroids are cheaters who do not deserve accolades for breaking records or winning at all costs will the doping stop. The Olympic Games are on the right track with the way athletes who are caught using performance-enhancing substances are disciplined: a two-year ban for the first offense and a lifetime ban if they are caught a second time. If sports fans are more interested in seeing sporting records fall, then they should push for the legalization of steroids and leave it up to the athlete to decide whether or not to use performance-enhancing drugs. Either way, society must change its cultural values.

NOTES

Introduction: A Commonly Used Drug

1. Rafael Palmeiro, Testimony before the House Committee on Government Reform, March 17, 2005. http://oversight.house .gov/features/steroids/testimony_palmeiro.PDF.
2. Quoted in Selena Roberts and David Epstein, "Confronting A-Rod," *Sports Illustrated*, February 16, 2009, p. 28.
3. Quoted in Peter Gammons, "Rodriguez: Sorry and Deeply Regretful," ESPN, February 9, 2009. http://sports.espn.go.com/ mlb/news/story?id=3895281.
4. Jose Canseco, *Vindicated: Big Names, Big Liars, and the Battle to Save Baseball*. New York: Simon Spotlight Entertainment, 2008, p. 148.
5. Jose Canseco, *Juiced: Wild Times, Rampant 'Roids, Smash Hits, and How Baseball Got Big*. New York: Regan, 2005, p. 170.
6. Canseco, *Vindicated*, pp. 130–31.
7. Canseco, *Vindicated*, p. 148.
8. George J. Mitchell, *Report to the Commissioner of Baseball of an Independent Investigation into the Illegal Use of Steroids and Other Performance-Enhancing Substances by Players in Major League Baseball*, Office of the Commissioner of Baseball, December 13, 2007, p. SR-8. http://files.mlb.com/mitchrpt.pdf.

Chapter 1: A Short History of the Use of Steroids in Sports

9. Jesse Haggard, *Demystifying Steroids*. Bloomington, IN: AuthorHouse, 2008, p. 14.
10. Quoted in WCHS-TV, "Steroids Treat Burns," April 10, 2002. www.wchstv.com/newsroom/healthyforlife/1877.shtml.
11. Quoted in John McCloskey and Julian Bailes, *When Winning Costs Too Much: Steroids, Supplements, and Scandal in Today's Sports*. Lanham, MD: Taylor Trade, 2005, p. 8.

12. Terry Todd, "The Steroid Predicament," *Sports Illustrated*, August 1, 1983. http://vault.sportsillustrated.cnn.com/vault/article/magazine/MAG1121081/3/index.htm.

13. Richard Pound, *Inside Dope: How Drugs Are the Biggest Threat to Sports, Why You Should Care, and What Can Be Done About Them*. Mississauga, ON: Wiley, 2006, p. 54.

14. Quoted in Michael Janofsky, "Coaches Concede That Steroids Fueled East Germany's Success in Swimming," *New York Times*, December 3, 1991, p. B15.

15. Quoted in Merrell Noden, "A Dirty Coach Comes Clean," *Sports Illustrated*, March 13, 1989, p. 22.

16. Quoted in Mike Fainaru-Wada, "Steroids' Powerful, Troubling Attraction," *San Francisco Chronicle*, July 8, 2004, p. B1.

17. Quoted in Fainaru-Wada, "Steroids' Powerful, Troubling Attraction," p B1.

18. Quoted in Fainaru-Wada, "Steroids' Powerful, Troubling Attraction," P. B1.

19. Quoted in Brent Schrotenboer, "Players of Substance," *San Diego Union-Tribune*, September 21, 2008. www.signon sandiego.com/uniontrib/20080921/news_1s21nflmai.html.

20. Schrotenboer, "Players of Substance."

21. Quoted in Schrotenboer, "Players of Substance."

22. Quoted in Jim Hoagland, "Summer of Skepticism," *Washington Post*, July 29, 2007, B7.

23. Quoted in Tom Verducci, "Totally Juiced," *Sports Illustrated*, June 3, 2002, p. 34.

24. Jose Canseco, *Juiced*, p. 237.

25. Quoted in Wayne Coffey, "Teens' Big Worry: For High School Athletes, Steroids Still the Rage," *New York Daily News*, December 16, 2007. www.nydailynews.com/sports/high_school/2007/12/16/2007-12-16_teens_big_worry_for_high_school_athletes.html.

Chapter 2: Why Use Steroids?

26. Quoted in McCloskey and Bailes, *When Winning Costs Too Much: Steroids, Supplements, and Scandal in Today's Sports*, p. 15.

27. Nathan Jendrick, *Dunks, Doubles, Doping: How Steroids Are Killing American Athletics*. Guilford, CT: Lyons, 2006, p. 26.

28. Jendrick, *Dunks, Doubles, Doping*, p. 26.
29. Quoted in Darla Atlas, "Teens Using Steroids Cheat Themselves and Their Health," *Dallas Morning News*, February 5, 2008. www.dallasnews.com/sharedcontent/dws/fea/lifetravel/stories/DN-nh_steroid_0205liv.ART.State.Edition1.45 67494.html.
30. Dan Clark, *Gladiator: A True Story of 'Roids, Rage, and Redemption.* New York: Scribner, 2009, pp. 32–33.
31. Canseco, *Juiced*, pp. 136–37.
32. Canseco, *Juiced*, p. 9.
33. Quoted in Tracy Wheeler, "Steroid Expert Says Teens Following Heroes' Lead," *Akron* (OH) *Beacon Journal*, March 8, 2008.
34. Quoted in Jessica Burkhart, "Scary Steroids," *Listen*, January 2008, p. 6.
35. Quoted in Brittany Stahl, "Despite MLB Scandals, Steroid Use Rampant in College Baseball," *NYC Pavement Pieces*, March 26, 2009. http://journalism.nyu.edu/pubzone/pavement/in/despite-mlb-scandals-steroids-rampant-in-college-baseball.
36. Stan Grossfeld, "When Cheers Turn to Depression," *Boston Globe*, February 19, 2008. www.boston.com/sports/schools/articles/2008/02/19/when_cheers_turn_to_depression.
37. Quoted in Grossfeld, "When Cheers Turn to Depression."
38. Anonymous, "True Stories of Steroid Abuse," Association Against Steroid Abuse. www.steroidabuse.com/true-stories-of-steroid-abuse.html.
39. Clark, *Gladiator*, p. 5.
40. Quoted in Kirsten Sparre, "Doping Harms the Children of Athletes," *Play the Game*, 2008, p. 3.
41. Giselher Spitzer and Sabra Lane, "Doped East German Athletes and Children Suffer Health Problems: Study," ABC Online, November 1, 2007. www.abc.net.au/am/content/2007/s2078111.htm.

Chapter 3: Is It Cheating to Use Steroids?

42. Dave Zirin, "Why Barry Bonds Is Not on Steroids," *Counterpunch*, March 27–28, 2004. www.counterpunch.org/zirin032 72004.html.

43. Michael Wilbon, "Tarnished Records Deserve an Asterisk," *Washington Post*, December 4, 2004, p. D10.

44. Canseco, *Juiced*, p. 2.

45. Wilbon, "Tarnished Records Deserve an Asterisk."

46. Quoted in Verducci, "Totally Juiced," p. 38.

47. Quoted in Fainaru-Wada and Williams, "Steroids' Powerful, Troubling Attraction," p. B1.

48. Alva Noe, "A-Rod Isn't a Cheater," Salon.com, May 1, 2009. www.salon.com/env/feature/2009/05/01/a_rod_steroids.

49. Randy Cohen, "Is Manny Ramirez Really All That Bad?" *New York Times*, May 19, 2009. http://ethicist.blogs.nytimes.com/2009/05/19/is-manny-ramirez-really-all-that-bad/?apage=2.

50. Cohen, "Is Manny Ramirez Really All That Bad?"

51. Quoted in Patrick Hruby, "Let the Juicing Begin," ESPN.com: Page 2, March 10, 2006. http://sports.espn.go.com/espn/page2/story?page=hruby/060310.

52. Quoted in Mary Crowley, ed., *From Birth to Death and Bench to Clinic: The Hastings Center Bioethics Briefing Book for Journalists, Policymakers, and Campaigns.* Garrison, NY: Hastings Center, 2008, p. 156.

53. Pound, *Inside Dope*, p. 12.

54. Joe Lindsey, "Why Legalizing Sports Doping Won't Work," *Freakonomics Blog, New York Times*, July 27, 2007. http://freakonomics.blogs.nytimes.com/2007/07/27/why-legalizing-sports-doping-wont-work/.

55. Pound, *Inside Dope*, p. 38.

56. Lindsey, *New York Times*, July 27, 2007.

Chapter 4: Regulating Steroid Use

57. Quoted in John Romano and Rick Collins, "Schedule 3—the Hard Way!" IronMagazine.com, April 16, 2009. www.ironmagazineforums.com/anabolic-zone/98714-anabolic-steroid-ban-explained.html.

58. Quoted in Mark Conrad, *The Business of Sports: A Primer for Journalists.* Mahwah, NJ: Lawrence Erlbaum, 2006, pp. 234–35.

59. Palmeiro, Testimony before the House Committee on Government Reform.

60. Quoted in Michael A. Hiltzik, "And Now, Is Baseball Serious?" *Los Angeles Times*, May 8, 2009, p. A1.

61. Quoted in Enrique Rangel, "HS Athletes Pass Steroids Test," *Lubbock* (TX) *Avalanche-Journal*, June 19, 2008. www.lubbockonline.com/stories/061908/loc_292671263.shtml.

62. Quoted in Geoff Mulvihill, "Few Caught by Steroid Testing in High School," StandardNET, March 17, 2009. www.standard.net/live/sports/prepinsider/167292.

63. Russell Meldrum and Judy Feinberg, "Drug Use by College Athletes: Is Testing an Effective Deterrent?" *Sport Journal*, Spring 2002. www.thesportjournal.org/article/drug-use-college-athletes-random-testing-effective-deterrent.

64. Quoted in Mulvihill, "Few Caught by Steroid Testing in High School."

65. Linn Goldberg, Testimony before the U.S. House of Representatives, Committee on Government Reform, April 27, 2005. http://oversight.house.gov/documents/20050427111957-63760.pdf.

Chapter 5: What Is the Future of Steroids in Sports?

66. Don Catlin and Peter Aldhouse, "Ending the Influence," *New Scientist*, August 11, 2007, p. 45.

67. Bill Romanowski and Adam Shefter, *Romo*. New York: HarperCollins, 2005, p. 7.

68. Quoted in Amy Shipley, "Chemists Stay a Step Ahead of Drug Testers," *Washington Post*, October 18, 2005, p. E1.

69. Jendrick, *Dunks, Doubles, Doping*, p. 162.

70. Jendrick, *Dunks, Doubles, Doping*, p. 163.

71. Quoted in Christa Case Bryant, "Gatekeeper for Clean Sports," *Christian Science Monitor*, August 4, 2008. http://features.csmonitor.com/backstory/2008/08/04/qdope4.

72. Quoted in Josh Peter and Charles Robinson, "Believe It or Not: Clean Team USA?" *Yahoo! Sports*, August 5, 2008. http://sports.yahoo.com/olympics/news?slug=ys-olympicdoping080508&prov=yhoo&type=lgns.

73. Quoted in Alice Park, "What's Driving Dara Torres," *Time*, August 4, 2008, p. 47.

74. Quoted in Park, "What's Driving Dara Torres," p. 47.

75. Quoted in Park, "What's Driving Dara Torres," p. 47.
76. *New York Times*, "Mark McGwire's Pep Pills," August 27, 1998, p. A22.
77. John Holberman, "Mark McGwire's Little Helper: The Androstenedione Debate," Think Muscle. www.thinkmuscle.com/articles/hoberman/mcgwire.htm.
78. Canseco, *Juiced*, p. 9.
79. Sanjay Gupta, "The Truth About Steroids and Sports," CBS News.com, February 3, 2008. www.cbsnews.com/stories/2008/02/03/sunday/main3783478.shtml.

DISCUSSION QUESTIONS

Chapter 1: A Short History of the Use of Steroids in Sports

1. Why do some athletes believe they must take steroids?
2. Why are clean athletes upset about athletes who take steroids and compete?
3. Why do people worry about the impact that athletes who take steroids will have on teens?

Chapter 2: Why Use Steroids?

1. How do the risks of steroid use differ in men and women?
2. According to Jose Canseco, why have most athletes considered using steroids?
3. What are some reasons why nonathletes take steroids, according to the author?

Chapter 3: Is It Cheating to Use Steroids?

1. Why do some fans and sportswriters believe athletes who use performance-enhancing substances should have an asterisk placed next to their sports statistics?
2. According to Jose Canseco, why are steroids good for baseball?
3. What is the moral and ethical difference, if any, between pharmaceutical performance enhancements and surgical enhancements?

Chapter 4: Regulating Steroid Use

1. How can sporting organizations enforce their ban on performance-enhancing substances?
2. Why did some government agencies oppose making steroids a Schedule III drug?
3. What does the WADA Anti-Doping Code mean when it says athletes are 100 percent responsible for banned substances found during drug tests?

Chapter 5: What Is the Future of Steroids in Sports?

1. How do the Clear and the Cream symbolize the difficulties inherent in testing for steroids?
2. Why do drug testers characterize drug tests as a never-ending game of catch-up?
3. What keeps WADA from guaranteeing the athletes in its Project Believe program are 100 percent clean?

ORGANIZATIONS TO CONTACT

Association Against Steroid Abuse (AASA)
521 N. Sam Houston Pkwy. E., Ste. 635
Houston, TX 77060
e-mail: www.steroidabuse.com

AASA is an educational organization that provides information and statistics on the dangers and issues of anabolic steroid abuse. Its Web site includes information about steroid abuse, steroids and sports, the law, steroid myths, steroids and women, and different steroids.

National Clearinghouse for Alcohol and Drug Information
PO Box 2345
Rockville, MD 20847-2345
phone: (301) 468-2600; (800) 729-6686
fax: (301) 468-6433
e-mail: shs@health.org
Web site: www.health.org

The clearinghouse distributes publications of the U.S. Department of Health and Human Services, the National Institute on Drug Abuse, and other federal agencies concerned with alcohol and drug abuse. It provides reports, fact sheets, posters, and videos on steroid abuse, prevention, and treatment. Some of the publications are available on its Web site; others may be ordered at low cost.

National Institute on Drug Abuse (NIDA)
6001 Executive Blvd.
Bethesda, MD 20892-9561
phone: (301) 443-1124; (888) 644-6432
e-mail: information@nida.nih.gov
Web site: www.steroidabuse.org

The NIDA supports and conducts research on drug abuse—including the yearly Monitoring the Future Survey—to improve drug abuse prevention, treatment, and policy efforts. It has a Web site devoted solely to anabolic steroid abuse, where it offers research reports and information about steroids. Information about steroids can also be found in its bimonthly *NIDA Notes* newsletter, the periodic *NIDA Capsules* fact sheets, and a catalog of research reports and public education materials, which can be found on the NIDA's home page at www.drugabuse.gov.

Office of National Drug Control Policy
Executive Office of the President
Drugs and Crime Clearinghouse
PO Box 6000
Rockville, MD 20849-6000
e-mail: ondcp@ncjrs.org
Web site: www.whitehousedrugpolicy.gov

The Office of National Drug Control Policy is responsible for formulating the government's national drug strategy and the president's anti-drug policy, as well as coordinating the federal agencies responsible for stopping drug trafficking. Information about anabolic androgenic steroids can be found on its Web site.

Oregon Health and Science University Center for Health Promotion and Sports Medicine
3181 S.W. Sam Jackson Park Rd.
Portland, OR 97239-3098
phone: (503) 418-4166
fax: (503) 494-1310
e-mail: chpr@ohsu.edu
Web site: www.ohsu.edu/hpsm/center.cfm

The Oregon Health and Science University Center for Health Promotion and Sports Medicine offers two educational programs for coaches and trainers in schools, who then lead the programs for their athletes. ATLAS, geared for male athletes, and ATHENA, for female athletes, provide substance-abuse prevention and information about healthy sports nutrition and strength training alternatives to illicit performance-enhancing drugs and alcohol.

Taylor Hooton Foundation
PO Box 2104
Frisco, TX 75034-9998
phone: (972) 403-7300
e-mail: don.hooton@taylorhooton.org
Web site: www.taylorhooton.org

Founded in memory of Taylor Hooton, a high school athlete who committed suicide shortly after coming off a cycle of steroids, the foundation provides information about the dangers of anabolic steroid abuse and emphasizes prevention. The Web site offers educational resources and shares the tragic experiences of users and their families.

U.S. Anti-Doping Agency (USADA)
2550 Tenderfoot Hill St., Ste. 200
Colorado Springs, CO 80906-7346
phone: (719) 785-2000; (866) 601-2632
Web site: www.usantidoping.org

The USADA is the national anti-doping organization for the U.S. Olympics, Paralympics, and Pan American Games. USADA is responsible for testing athletes involved in these games for banned substances. Its anti-doping program researches banned substances. USADA also offers an educational program to inform athletes, coaches, and trainers about policies, procedures, athletes' rights and responsibilities, and the dangers and consequences of using banned substances in sports.

World Anti-Doping Agency (WADA)
800 Place Victoria, Ste. 1700
PO Box 120
Montreal, Quebec CANADA H4Z 1B7
phone: (514) 904-9232
fax: (514) 904-8650
e-mail: info@wada-ama.org
Web site: www.wada-ama.org

The WADA is an international independent organization created to promote, coordinate, and monitor the fight against doping in sports. It developed the World Anti-Doping Code, which sets anti-doping policies, procedures, and regulations for all its participating nations. The code also includes the list of prohibited substances, exemptions for therapeutic use, rules for testing athletes, and protections for protecting athletes' privacy.

FOR MORE INFORMATION

Books

Jacqueline Adams, *Steroids*. Farmington Hills, MI: Lucent, 2006. A thorough examination of the issues involved with steroids.

Jose Canseco, *Juiced: Wild Times, Rampant 'Roids, Smash Hits, and How Baseball Got Big*. New York: Regan, 2005. The former major leaguer writes a tell-all book about steroid use in baseball and names other players he claims used steroids.

Dan Clark, *Gladiator: A True Story of 'Roids, Rage, and Redemption*. New York: Scribner, 2009. The American Gladiator Nitro tells his story about how he came to use steroids, what his life was like on steroids, and how he eventually quit using them.

Laura K. Egendorf, *Compact Research: Performance-Enhancing Drugs*. San Diego: ReferencePoint, 2007. An overview of pro and con viewpoints on performance-enhancing drugs, with primary source quotations, facts, and illustrations.

Mike Fainaru-Wada and Lance Williams, *Game of Shadows: Barry Bonds, BALCO, and the Steroids Scandal That Rocked Professional Sports*. New York: Gotham, 2006. The complete exposé of the BALCO steroid scandal that implicated so many athletes, by the journalists who first broke the story.

Louise Gerdes, *At Issue: Performance Enhancing Drugs*. Farmington Hills, MI: Greenhaven, 2008. A collection of articles presenting both pro and con viewpoints on performance-enhancing drugs.

Nathan Jendrick, *Dunks, Doubles, Doping: How Steroids Are Killing American Athletics*. Guilford, CT: Lyons, 2006. Argues that steroids are not necessarily doing the most damage to American athletics; it is the hype, misleading information, and inconsistencies in policy that are most harmful to sports.

Richard Pound, *Inside Dope: How Drugs Are the Biggest Threat to Sports, Why You Should Care, and What Can Be Done About Them.* Mississauga, ON: Wiley, 2006. Tackles the issue of doping in sports: why it is a problem, how coaches, doctors, and trainers are involved, and the drug test battle to stay ahead of the users.

Periodicals

Peter Aldhous, "Inside the Minds of Athletes Who Cheat," *New Scientist*, August 2, 2008. Finding out why some competitors take drugs while others stay clean may be the key to deterring doping.

Marky Billson, "Cheating in Baseball Is Old News," *Baseball Digest*, May 2008. Players have been cheating in baseball since the time the game was invented.

Randy Cohen, "Is Manny Ramirez Really All That Bad?" *New York Times*, May 19, 2009. A look at how sports evolve and whether it is right to ban performance-enhancing drugs and not surgical enhancements.

David Epstein, "The Rules, the Law, the Reality," *Sports Illustrated*, February 16, 2009. A review of baseball's steroid policy through the years.

Michael Hiltzik, "Athletes, Steroids, and Public Hysteria," *Los Angeles Times*, March 2, 2009. A discussion of what sports organizations and drug testing companies should do about steroids in sports.

Alice Park, "What's Driving Dara Torres," *Time*, August 4, 2008. The forty-one-year-old Olympic medalist wants to compete in her fifth Olympics and is willing to take drug tests to prove she's better than ever without drugs.

Marissa Saltzman, "Chemical Edge: The Risks of Performance-Enhancing Drugs," *Odyssey*, May 2006. Argues that performance-enhancing drugs should not have a place in sports.

Kate Schmidt, "Steroids: Take One for the Team," *Los Angeles Times*, October 14, 2007. An Olympic medalist argues that steroids should be legalized and allowed in sports.

Abraham Socher, "No Game for Old Men," *Commentary*, March 2008. It is suspicious when athletes hit their prime in their thirties or forties; most athletes have the best years of their career in their twenties.

Internet Sources

Joe Lindsey, "Is There Another Way to Eliminate Doping?" *New York Times Freakonomics Blog*, January 29, 2008. http://freako nomics.blogs.nytimes.com/2007/07/27/why-legalizing-sports-doping-wont-work/. Professional bicycle racing is starting a new comprehensive anti-doping program that will test every rider before the race starts to look for signs of doping.

George J. Mitchell, *Report to the Commissioner of Baseball of an Independent Investigation into the Illegal Use of Steroids and Other Performance Enhancing Substances by Players in Major League Baseball*, Office of the Commissioner of Baseball. December 13, 2007. http://files.mlb.com/mitchrpt.pdf. The Mitchell Report is a comprehensive look at the use of steroids in Major League Baseball.

U.S. Senate Committee on Foreign Relations, "International Convention Against Doping in Sport," May 22, 2008. http://foreign .senate.gov/hearings/2008/hrg080522a.html. A Senate hearing on steroid use in athletics with testimony from members of the U.S. Olympic Committee and the U.S. Anti-Doping Agency.

Web Sites

Steroid Abuse (www.steroid-abuse.org). Designed by a group of steroid users and sports medicine doctors, the Web site attempts to dispel the myths of steroid use while providing comprehensive information on how to stop steroid abuse.

Steroid Law (www.steroidlaw.com). Criminal attorney and former bodybuilder Rick Collins believes the health risks of steroids are exaggerated. His Web site provides health and legal information about steroids and advocates the reform of current steroid laws.

Steroid Nation (http://grg51.typepad.com/steroid_nation). An online journal that examines the use of anabolic steroids and other performance-enhancing drugs in sports, youth, and society, written by physician Gary Gaffney from the University of Iowa, College of Medicine.

Films

Bigger, Stronger, Faster. Directed by Christopher Bell. Magnolia Home Entertainment, 2008, DVD. A documentary that offers a personal look at steroid use among athletes, told by a wrestler who chose not to take steroids while his two brothers did.

INDEX

A
Aaron, Hank, 42
Acne, 36, *37*
American Medical
  Association (AMA), 59
Anabolic Steroid Control
  Act (1990), 57
Androstenedione, 6, 65,
86
Anti-Doping Code (World
  Anti-Doping Agency), 60
  Anti-Drug Abuse Act
    (1988), 57
  steroids give unfair
    advantage, 45–46, 49
Arnold, Patrick, 77
Assael, Shaun, 86
ATHENA program, 34,
  72–73
Athletes
  influence on teen athletes,
    33
  methods of steroid use by,
    27–28
  penalties for steroid use
    by, 58, 80
  public attitudes on use of
    steroids by, 86–87
  steroids as natural

enhancements for, 49,
  51–52
steroids give unfair
  advantage, 45–46, 49
ATLAS program, 34, 72–73

B
BALCO (Bay Area
  Laboratory Co-Operative)
  scandal, 75–78, 79, 80
Bartle, Matt, 71–72
Baseball. *See* Major League
  Baseball
Basketball. *See* National
  Basketball Association
Basso, Ivan, 20
Berning, Joseph, 33
Birth defects, 40–41
Bonds, Barry, 32, 42–43,
  44, 76
  home run record
    before/after steroid use,
    9
  testimony on BALCO
    scandal, 44
Bosworth, Brian, 24
Brown-Séquard,
  Charles-Édouard, 19
Burn patients, 2–13, *12*

C
Caminiti, Ken, 20–21, 45
Canseco, Jose, 22
    on steroid use in, 8, 9,
        21–22, 31–32, 67, 87
    on steroids as good for
        baseball, 43, 45
Castellanos, Kris, 32, 35
Catlin, Don H., 74–75, 75,
    76, 82, 83–84
Centers for Disease Control
    and Prevention (CDC),
    23
Chambers, Dwain, 76
Chavoor, Sherm, 16
Clark, Dan, 29–30, 36–37,
    62
Clay, Brian, 84
College athletes, steroid use
    among, 24
Condin, Timothy, 82
Conte, Victor, 76, 77, 77,
    78, 79
Cooper, Chris, 76
Cycling, steroid use in,
    20

D
Demystifying Steroids
    (Haggard), 11
Diamond Blackfan anemia,
    13
Dianabol, 14–15
Dunks, Doubles, Doping
    (Jendrick), 26, 82–83

E
Ewing, Jack, 70

F
Fainaru-Wada, Mark, 48,
    48
Feinberg, Judy, 72
Ferrando, Amy, 13
Ferstle, Jim, 87
Florida, high school drug
    testing in, 70, 71
Flynn, Dan, 71
Football. See National
    Football League
Francis, Charlie, 17–18
Frick, Ford, 42
Friedman, Jackie, 63
Fuentes, Eufemiano, 20

G
Giambi, Jason, 76
Gladiator (Clark), 36–37
Goldberg, Linn, 34, 34, 72,
    73
Graham, Trevor, 75–76
Griesemer, Bernard, 33
Gupta, Sanjay, 87
Gynecomastia, 36, 40

H
Haggard, Jesse, 11, 24
Hoberman, John, 86–87
Hockey. See National
    Hockey League
Hoffman, Bob, 14, 15

Human growth hormone (hGH), 6
  medical uses for, 13
  risks of, 17
  safety of, 14

I
Illinois, high school drug testing in, 71
Inside Dope (Pound), 52–53
International Association of Athletics Foundation, 55, 76

J
Jacobs, Regina, 76
Jendrick, Nathan, 26, 28, 82–83
Johnson, Ben, *56,* 57, 59
Jones, Marion, 79, *79,* 80
Juiced (Canseco), 8, 21–22, 87

K
Kidneys, 38
Klatz, Ronald M., 14

L
Landis, Floyd, 20, *21*
Langston, Edward, 59
LeMond, Greg, 20
LePage, Michael, 33
Lindsey, Joe, 53–54
Liver, 38, *39*

M
Major League Baseball (MLB), 6, 63, 65
  commissioner of, 69
  debate over antidrug policy of, 67–68
  Mitchell report on, 9–10
  penalties for performance-enhancing drug use in, 58
Maley, Mark, 32
Maris, Roger, 42
McEwen, John, 76
McGwire, Mark, 6, 8, 9, 46, 86
Media
  coverage of Mark McGwire's steroid use, 86–87
  promotes steroid look, 34
Meldrum, Russell, 72
Mitchell, George J., 9, *10*
Mitchell Report (2007), 9–10, 22–23, 69
Monitoring the Future survey, 70
Murray, Thomas H., 52

N
National Basketball Association (NBA), 62–63
  penalties for performance-enhancing drug use in, 58

National Collegiate Athletic
  Association (NCAA), 24
National Football League
  (NFL)
    penalties for performance-
      enhancing drug use in, 58
    steroid use in, 19–20
National Hockey League
  (NHL),
    penalties for performance-
      enhancing drug use in,
      58
National Institute on Drug
  Abuse (NIDA), 72–73
Nelson, Adam, 18–19
New Jersey, high school
  drug testing in, 71
Nieboer, Dan, 29
Noe, Alva, 49
Norethandrolone, 74

O
Olympic Games
  first documented use of
    steroids in, 14
  includes steroids in list of
    banned substances, 55,
    57
  penalties for performance-
    enhancing drug use in,
    58, 80
  use of steroids in, 15–17

P
Palmeiro, Rafael, 6, 65

Patrick, Danica, 59
Perls, Tom, 17
Phelps, Michael, 84
Pound, Richard, 16, 45,
  52–53, 54
  on athletes claiming never
    to have tested positive,
    83
  on cheating on steroid
    tests, 65
Price, Melissa, 76
Project Believe (U.S. Anti-
  Doping Agency), 84, 86

R
Ramirez, Manny, 6, 7, 23,
  67–68
Roberts, Dionne, 35
Rodriguez, Alex, 7, 7–8
'Roid rage, 39
Romanowski, Bill, 38, 76,
  80, 81, 82
Ruth, Babe, 42

S
San Diego Union-Tribune
  (newspaper), 19
San Francisco Chronicle
  (newspaper), 48
Schilling, Curt, 46
Selig, Bud, 9, 69, 69
Sheffield, Gary, 76
Side effects, 14, 36, 38–39
  in women, 40–41
Sosa, Sammy, 6, 9, 46

Sports Illustrated (magazine), 7, 21

Sptiz, Mark, 16

Steroid Nation (Assael), 86

Steroids
anabolic *vs.* androgenic, 11
availability of, 24–25
bans on, 55, 57
development of undetectable types, 74–75, 79–80, 82–83
first use in athletic competition, 14
medical uses for, 11–13, 26–27
as natural enhancements, 49, 51–52
opposition to regulation of, 58–59
prevalence of use among youth, 70
public attitudes on use by athletes, 86–87
use at Olympic Games, 15–17
use in cycling, 20, 59–60, 70
use in professional baseball, 8–9, 20–23, 31–32
use in professional football, 19–20
See also Side effects; Testing

T

Taylor, William N., 29

Teenagers
in athletics, pressures on to use steroids, 33, 35, 72–73
media promotes steroid look among, 35
steroid use among, 23–24, 26
testing of, in high school/college, 68, 70–71

Tennant, Forrest, 19

Testing, for performance-enhancing drugs
alternatives to, 83–84
cheating on, 65
in high school/college, 68, 70–71
as never-ending game of catch-up, 82–83
testosterone-epitestosterone ratio in, 78

Testosterone
effects of estrogen on production of, 36
first isolation of, 11
prostate cancer and, 23, 24, 38
ratio to epitestosterone, 78
in treatment of burn patients, 12–13

Tetrahydrogestrinone
  (THG), 38, 76–77
Texas, high school drug
  testing in, 70, 71, 72
Thomas, Tammy, 74
Todd, Terry, 15
Torres, Dara, 84, *85*, 86
Toth, Kevin, 76
Tour de France, 20, 59–60,
  61, 70
Trammel, Terrence, 78
Tygart, Travis, 80, 84,
  86

U
Ullrich, Jan, 20
U.S. Anti-Doping Agency
  (USADA), 75

V
Voy, Robert, 26

W
Wadler, Gary I., 67, *68*
Walker, Dan, 32
Wanninger, Rich, 76

Washington Post
  (newspaper), 82
Weight lifter(s), 15
  discovery of steroids by,
    13–14
Wheatley, Tyrone, 76
White, Kelli, 76
Wilbon, Michael, 42
Williams, Lance, 48, *48*
Women, side effects of
  steroid use in, 40–41
Woods, Tiger, 49
World Anti-Doping Agency
  (WADA), 16, 60
World Wrestling
  Federation, 62

Y
Yesalis, Charles, 18, 20
Youth Risk Behavior Survey
  (Centers for Disease
  Control and Prevention),
  23

Z
Ziegler, John, 14

PICTURE CREDITS

ABOUT THE AUTHOR

Tamara L. Roleff has been working as an editor and writer for what seems like forever. She and her husband, Keith, now live in Southern California after traveling the world thanks to the U.S. Marine Corps. When she is not writing or editing books, she likes to travel with the love of her life, train and show her golden retrievers in agility and obedience, hang out in the pool, read mystery books, and play mah-jongg with friends.